# THE

# CHALDEAN

# ORACLES

## G. R. S. Mead

ISBN 1-56459-250-2

# ECHOES FROM THE GNOSIS.

Under this general title is now being published a series of small volumes, drawn from, or based upon, the mystic, theosophic and gnostic writings of the ancients, so as to make more easily audible for the ever-widening circle of those who love such things, some echoes of the mystic experiences and initiatory lore of their spiritual ancestry. There are many who love the life of the spirit, and who long for the light of gnostic illumination, but who are not sufficiently equipped to study the writings of the ancients at first hand, or to follow un-aided the labours of scholars. These little volumes are therefore intended to serve as introduction to the study of the more difficult literature of the subject; and it is hoped that at the same time they may become for some, who have as yet not even heard of the Gnosis, stepping-stones to higher things.

G. R. S. M.

# THE CHALDÆAN ORACLES.

## VOLUME I.

## CONTENTS.

## BIBLIOGRAPHY.

*K.* = Kroll (G.), *De Oraculis Chaldaicis;* in *Breslauer philologische Abhandlungen*, Bd. vii., Hft. 1. (Breslau ; 1894).

*C.* = Cory (I. P.), *Ancient Fragments* (London ; 2nd ed., 1832), pp. 239—280.  The first and third editions do not contain the text of our Oracles.

*F.* = Mead (G. R. S.), *Fragments of a Faith Forgotten* (London ; 2nd. ed., 1906).

*H.* = Mead (G. R. S.), *Thrice Greatest Hermes* (London ; 1906).

# THE CHALDÆAN ORACLES.

## INTRODUCTION.

The Chaldæan Oracles (*Lógia, Oracula, Responsa*) are a product of Hellenistic (and more precisely Alexandrian) syncretism.

The Alexandrian religio-philosophy proper was a blend of Orphic, Pythagoræan, Platonic, and Stoic elements, and constituted the theology of the learned in the great city which had gradually, from the third century B.C., made herself the centre of Hellenic culture.

In her intimate contact with the Orient, the mind of Greece freely united with the mysterious and enthusiastic cults and wisdom-traditions of the other nations, and became very industrious in " philosophizing " their mythology, theosophy and gnosis, their oracular utterances, symbolic apocalypses and initiatory lore.

The two nations that made the deepest impression on the Greek thinkers were Egypt and Chaldæa; these they regarded as the possessors of the most ancient wisdom-traditions.

How Hellenism philosophized the ancient wisdom of Egypt, we have already shown at great length in our volumes on Thrice-greatest Hermes. The Chaldæan Oracles are a parallel endeavour, on a smaller scale, to philosophize the wisdom of Chaldæa. In the Trismegistic writings, moreover, we had to deal with a series of prose treatises, whereas in our Oracles we are to treat of the fragments of a single mystery-poem, which may with advantage be compared with the cycle of Jewish and Christian pseudepigraphic poems known as the Sibylline Oracles.

The Great Library of Alexandria contained a valuable collection of MSS. of what we may term the then "Sacred Books of the East " in their original tongues. Many of these were translated, and among them the "Books of the Chaldæans." Thus Zosimus, the early alchemist, and a member of one of the later Trismegistic communities, writes, somewhere at the end of the third century A.D. :

" The Chaldæans and Parthians and Medes and Hebrews call him [the First Man] Adam, which is by interpretation virgin Earth, and blood-red Earth, and fiery Earth, and fleshly Earth.

" And these indications were found in the book-collections of the Ptolemies, which they stored away in every temple, and especially in the Serapeum " (*H.*, iii., 277).

The term Chaldæan is, of course, vague, and scientifically inaccurate. Chaldæan is a Greek synonym for Babylonian, and is the way they transliterated the Assyrian name Kaldū. The land of the Kaldū proper lay S.E. of Babylonia proper on what was then the sea-coast. As the *Encyclopædia Biblica* informs us :

11

**THE CHALDÆAN ORACLES.**

"The Chaldæans not only furnished an early dynasty of Babylon, but also were incessantly pressing into Babylonia ; and, despite their repeated defeats by Assyria, they gradually gained the upper hand there. The founder of the New Babylonian Kingdom, Nabopolassar (*circa* 626 B.C.), was a Chaldæan, and from that time Chaldæa meant Babylonia. . . .

"We find 'Chaldæans' used in *Daniel*, as a name for a caste of wise men. As Chaldæan meant Babylonian in the wider sense of a member of the dominant race in the times of the new Babylonian Empire, so after the Persian conquest it seems to have connoted the Babylonian *literati* and became a synonym of soothsayer and astrologer. In this sense it passed into classical writers."

We shall, however, see from the fragments of our poem that some of the Chaldæi were something more than soothsayers and astrologers.

As to our sources; the *disjecta membra* of this lost mystery-poem are chiefly found in the books and commentaries of the Platonici—that is, of the Later Platonic school. In addition to this there are extant five treatises of the Byzantine period, dealing directly with the doctrines of the " Chaldæan philosophy " : five chapters of a book of Proclus, three treatises of Psellus (eleventh century), and a letter of a contemporary letter-writer, following on Psellus.

But by far the greatest number of our fragments is found in the books of the Later Platonic philosophers, who from the time of Porphyry (*fl. c.* 250-300)—and, therefore, we may conclude from that of Plotinus, the corypheus of the school— held these Oracles in the highest estimation. Almost without a break, the succession of the Chain praise and comment elaborately on them, from Porphyry onwards—Iamblichus, Julian the Emperor, Synesius, Syrianus, Proclus, Hierocles— till the last group who flourished in the first half of the sixth century, when Simplicius, Damascius and Olympiodorus

B 13

were still busy with the philosophy of our Oracles.

Some of them—Porphyry, Iamblichus and Proclus—wrote elaborate treatises on the subject; Syrianus wrote a " symphony " of Orpheus, Pythagoras and Plato with reference to and in explanation of the Oracles; while Hierocles, in his treatise *On Providence*, endeavoured to bring the doctrine of the Oracles into " symphony " with the dogmas of the Theurgists and the philosophy of Plato. All these books are, unfortunately, lost, and we have to be content with the scattered, though numerous, references, with occasional quotations, in such of their other works as have been preserved to us.

In this brief introduction it would take too long to discuss the " literature " of the Oracles; and indeed this is all the more unnecessary as until the work of Kroll appeared, the subject had never been treated scientifically. Prior to Kroll it had been, more or less, generally

14

held that the Oracles were a collection of sayings deriving immediately from the Chaldæan wisdom, and even by some as direct translations or paraphrases from a Chaldæan original.

This was the general impression made by the vagueness with which the Later Platonic commentators introduced their authority; as, for instance: The Chaldæan Oracles, the Chaldæans, the Assyrians, the Foreigners (*lit.*, Barbarians or Natives), the God-transmitted Wisdom, or Mystagogy handed on by the Gods; and, generally, simply: The Oracles, the Oracle, the Gods, or one of the Gods.

Kroll has been the first to establish that for all this there was but a single authority—namely, a poem in hexameter verse, in the conventional style of Greek Oracular utterances, as is the case with the Sibyllines and Homeric centones.

The fragments of this poem have, for the most part, been preserved to us by being embedded in a refined stratum of elaborate commentary, in which the simple forms of the poetical imagery and the symbolic expressions of the original have been blended with the subtleties of a highly developed and abstract systematization, which is for the most part foreign to the enthusiastic and vital spirit of the mystic utterances of the poem.

To understand the doctrines of the original poem, we must recover the fragments that remain, and piece them together as best we can under general and natural headings ; we must not, as has previously been done, content ourselves with reading them through the eyes of the philosophers of the Later Platonic School, whose one pre-occupation was not only to make a "harmony" or "symphony" between Orpheus, Pythagoras, Plato and the Oracles, but also to wrest the latter into accommodation with their own elaborations of Platonic and Plotinian doctrine.

When we have done this, we shall have before us the remains of a mystery-poem, addressed to "initiates," and evidently forming part of the inner instruction of a School or Community; but even so we shall not have the clear original, for there are several interpolations, which have crept in with the tradition of the text from hand to hand of many scribes.

What is the date of this original poem? It was known to Porphyry. Now Porphyry (Malek) was a Semite by birth and knew Hebrew; he may also have known "Chaldæan." At any rate we know he was a good scholar and had good critical ability, and that he was at pains to sift out "genuine" from spurious "Oracles," thus showing that there were many Oracles circulating in his day. The genuine ones he collected in his lost work entitled, *On the Philosophy of the Oracles*, and among them was our poem.

Kroll places this poem at the end of the second century or the beginning of the third, chiefly because it breathes the spirit of a " saving cult," and such cults, he believes, did not come into general prominence till the days of Marcus Aurelius (*imp.* 161-180). But saving cults had been a common-place of the East and in Alexandria for centuries, and this, therefore, does not seem to me to afford us any indication of date.

The two Julians, father and son, moreover, the former of whom Suidas calls a " Chaldæan philosopher," and the latter " the Theurgist," adding that the son flourished under Marcus Aurelius, will hardly help us in this connection ; for the father wrote a book *On Daimones* only, and, though the son wrote works on theurgy and also on the oracles of theurgy and the " secrets of this science," Porphyry did not associate him with our Oracles, for he devoted a separate book of commentaries (now lost) to " The Doctrines of Julian the Chaldæan," while Proclus and Damascius dissociate this Julian from our Oracles, by quoting him separately under the title " The Theurgist " (K. 71).

Porphyry evidently considered our THE CHALDÆAN ORACLES. Oracles as old, but how old? To this we can give no precise answer. The problem is the same as that which confronts us in both the Trismegistic and Sibylline literature, which can be pushed back in an unbroken line to the early years of the Ptolemaic period. We are, therefore, justified in saying that our poem may as easily be placed in the first as in the second century.

It remains only to be remarked that, as might very well be expected with such scattered shreds and fragments of highly poetical imagery and symbolic and mystical poetry, the task of translation is often very arduous, all the more so owing to the absence of truly critical texts of the documents from which they are recovered. Kroll has supplied us with an excellent apparatus and many emendations of the tradition of the printed texts; but until the extant works of the Later Platonic School are critically edited from the MSS. (as has been done only in a few instances) a truly critical text of our Oracle-fragments is out of the question. Kroll has printed all the texts, both of the fragments and of the contexts, in the ancient authors, where they are found, in his indispensable treatise in Latin on the subject, but, as is usual with the work of specialists, he does not translate a single line. With these brief remarks we now present the reader with a translation and comments on the fragments of what might be called " The Gnosis of the Fire."

# FRAGMENTS AND COMMENTS.

## THE SUPREME PRINCIPLE.

In the extant fragments of our Oracle-poem the Supreme Principle is characterized simply as Father, or Mind, or Mind of the Father, or again as Fire.

Psellus, however, in his commentary, declares that the Oracles hymned the Source of all as the One and Good (K. 10); and there can be little doubt that in the circle of our poet, the Deity was either regarded as the "One and All"—according to the grand formula of Heraclitus (*fl.* 500 B.C.), who had probably to some extent already "philosophized" the intuitions and symbols of a Mago-Chaldæan tradition—or, as with so many Gnostic schools of the time, was conceived of as the Ineffable.

Cory, in his collection of Oracle-fragments, includes (C. 1) a definition of the Supreme which Eusebius attributed to the " Persian Zoroaster." This may very well have been derived from some Hellenistic document influenced by the " Books of the Chaldæans," or " Books of the Medes," and may, therefore, be considered as generally consonant with the basic doctrine of our Oracles. As, however, Kroll rightly omits this, we append it in illustration only :

"He is the First, indestructible, eternal, ingenerable, impartible, entirely unlike aught else, Disposer of all beauty, unbribable, of all the good the Best, of all the wisest the Most Wise ; the Father of good-rule and righteousness is He as well, self-taught, and natural, perfect, and wise, the sole Discoverer of sacred nature-lore."

THE END OF UNDERSTANDING.

If, however, we have no excerpt bearing directly on the Summum Mysterium, we have enough, and more than enough, to support us in our conjecture that it was conceived of in our Oracles as being itself beyond all words, in a fragment of eleven lines which sets forth the supreme end of contemplation as follows :

*Yea, there is That which is the End-of-understanding, the That which thou must understand with flower of mind.*

K. 11.
C. 163.
167.

*For should'st thou turn thy mind inwards on It, and understand It as understanding " something," thou shalt not understand It.*

61.
62.
166.

*For that there is a power of [the mind's] prime that shineth forth in all directions, flashing with intellectual rays [lit., sectors].*

*Yet, in good sooth, thou should'st not [strive] with vehemence [to] understand that End-of-understanding, nor even with the wide-extended flame of wide-extended mind that measures all things—except that End-of-understanding [only].*

*Indeed there is no need of strain in understanding This; but thou should'st*

23

*have the vision of thy soul in purity, turned
from aught else, so as to make thy mind,
empty [of all things else], attentive to that
End, in order that thou mayest learn that
End-of-understanding ; for It subsists
beyond the mind.*

The " That which is the End-of-understanding " is generally rendered the Intelligible. But *to noētón*, for the Gnostic
of this tradition, in this connection
signifies the Self-creative Mind, that is,
the Mind that creates its own understanding.

It is both the simultaneous beginning
and end, or cause and result of itself ;
and thus is the end or goal of all understanding. It has, therefore, to be distinguished from all formal modes of
intellection ; the normal mind that is
conditioned by the opposites, subject
and object, cannot grasp it. So long as
we conceive it as object, as other than
ourselves, as though we are " understanding 'something,' " so long are we

24

without it. It must be contemplated with the " flower of mind," by mind in its " prime," that is, at the moment of blossoming of the growing mind, which rays within and without in intellectual brilliance, both penetrating its own depths and becoming one with them.

" Flower of mind," however, is not the fruit or jewels of mind, though it is a power of fiery mind, for flowers are on the sun-side of things. To understand " with flower of mind " thus seems to suggest to catch, like petals, in a cup-like way, with the *kratēres* or deeps of mind, the true fiery intelligence of the Great Mind, as flowers catch the sun-rays, and by means of them to bring to birth within oneself the fruit or jewels of the Mind, which are of the nature of immediate or spiritual understanding, that is to say, the greater mind-senses, or powers of understanding.

The fragment seems to be an instruction in a method of initiating the mind in understanding or true gnosis—a very subtle process. It is not to be expected that the normal, formal, partial mind can seize a complete idea, a fullness, as it erroneously imagines it does in the region of form ; in the living intelligible " spheres " there are no such limited ideas defined by form or outline ; they are measureless.

In this symbolism flame and flower are much the same ; flame of mind and flower of mind suggest the same happening in the " mineral " and " vegetable " kingdoms of the mind-realms. The mind has to grow of itself towards its sun. Most men's minds are at best smouldering fire ; they require a " breath " of the Great Breath to make them burst into flame, and so extend themselves, or possess themselves of new re-generative power. Most men's minds, or persons, are unripe plants ; we have not yet brought ourselves to the blossoming point. This is achieved only by Heat from the Sun. A blossoming person may be said to be one who is beginning to know how to form fruit and re-generate himself.

In this vital exercise of inner growth there must be no formal thinking. The personal mind must be made empty or void of all preconceptions, but at the same time become keenly attentive, transformed into pure sense, or capacity for greater sensations. The soul must be in a searching frame of mind, searching not enquiring, that is to say synthetic not analytic. Enquiry suggests penetrating into a thing with the personal mind ; while searching denotes embracing and seizing ideas, " eating " or " digesting " or " absorbing " them, so to say ; getting all round them and making them one's own, surrounding them—it is no longer a question of separated subject and object as with the personal and analyzing mind.

## MYSTIC UNION.

The whole instruction might be termed a method of *yoga* or mystic union (*unio*

27

*mystica*) of the spiritual or kingly mind, the mind that rules itself—*rāja-yoga*, the royal art proper. But there must be no " vehemence " (no " fierce impetuosity," to use a phrase of Patañjali's in his *Yoga-sūtra*) in one direction only ; there must be expansion in every direction within and without in stillness.

The " vision " of the soul is, literally, the " eye " of the soul. The mind must be emptied of every object, so that it may receive the fullness. It becomes the " pure eye," the æon, all-eye ; not, however, to perceive anything other than itself, but to understand the nature of understanding—namely, that it transcends all distinctions of subject and object.

And yet though the Reality may be said to be " beyond the mind," or " without it," it is really not so. It may very well be said to be beyond or transcend the personal or formal mind, or mind in separation, for that is the mind that separates ; but the Intelligible and

28

the Mind-in-itself are really one. As one of the fragments says :

*For Mind is not without the That-which-makes-it-Mind ; and That-which-is-the-End-of-Mind doth not subsist apart from Mind.*    K. 11. C. 43. 44.

Both these hyphened terms represent the same word in Greek, usually rendered the Intelligible. The Oracle might thus be made to run : " For Intellect is not without the Intelligible, and the Intelgible subsists not apart from Intellect." But this makes *to noētón* the object only of understanding ; whereas it is neither subject nor object, but both.

### THE ONE DESIRABLE.

The Father is the Source of all sources and the End of all ends ; He is the One Desirable, Perfect and Benignant, the Good, the Summum Bonum, as we learn from the following three disconnected fragments.

*K.* 15.     *For from the Paternal Source naught*
*C.*  9.     *that's imperfect spins* [or *wheels*].

The soul must have measure, rhythm, and perfection, to spin, circulate or throb with this Divine Principle.

*K.* 15.     *The Father doth not sow fear, but*
*C.* 10.     *pours forth persuasion.*

The Father controls from within and not from without ; controls by *being*, by living within, and not by constraining.

*K.* 15.     *Not knowing that God is wholly Good.*
*C.* 184.     *O wretched slaves, be sober !*

Compare with this the address of the preacher inserted in the Trismegistic " Man-Shepherd " treatise (*H.*, ii. 17) :
" O ye people, earth-born folk, ye who have given yourselves to drunkenness and sleep and ignorance of God, be sober now ! "
And also the Oracle quoted as follows :

30

*The soul of men shall press God closely*   K. 48.
*to itself, with naught subject to death in it ;*   C. 83.
*[but now] it is all drunk, for it doth glory*
*in the Harmony* [that is, *the Sublunary*
*or Fate Spheres*] *beneath whose sway the*
*mortal frame exists.*

## THE DIVINE TRIAD.

How the Divine Simplicity conditions
its self-revelation no fragment tells us.
But in spite of Kroll's scepticism I
believe the Later Platonic commentators
were not wrong when they sought for
it in the riddle of the triad or trinity.

The doctrine of the Oracles as to the
Self-conditioning of the Supreme Monad
may, however, perhaps, be recovered
from the passage of the Simonian *Great
Announcement* quoted in our last little
volume (pp. 40 ff). This striking ex-
position of the Gnosis was "philosophized" upon a Mago-Chaldæan back-
ground, and that, too, at a date at least
contemporaneous with the very origins
of Christianity, as is now, I think,

31

demonstrated with high probability (*H.,* i. 184). The passage is so important that it deserves re-quotation ; but as it is so easily accessible, it may be sufficient simply to refer the interested reader to it.

Centuries before Proclus this tripartite or triadic dogma was known to the Greeks as pre-eminently Assyrian, that is Syrian or Chaldæan. Thus Hippolytus, commenting on the Naassene Document, in which the references to the Initiatory Rites are pre-Christian, writes :

" And first of all, in considering the triple division of Man [the Monad or Logos], they [the Naassenes] fly for help to the Initiations of the Assyrians ; for the Assyrians were the first to consider the Soul triple and yet one " (*H.,* i. 151).

In the same Document the early Jewish commentator, who was in all probability a contemporary of Philo's in the earliest years of the Christian era, gives the first words of a mystery-hymn which run : " *From Thee* is Father and *Through Thee* Mother " (*ibid.,* 146) ; and,

32

it might be added: "*To Thee* is Son." This represents the values of the three "Great Names" on the Path of Return; but in the Way of Descent, that is of cosmogenesis, or world-shaping, their values would differ. Curiously enough one of our Oracles reads:

*For Power is* With Him, *but Mind* From Him.

K. 13.
C. 16.

Power always represents the Mother-side (the Many), the Spouse of Deity (the Mind, the One), and Son is the Result, the "From Him"—the Mind in manifestation. Hence we read of the Father, or Mind Proper, as becoming unmanifested or withdrawn, or hidden, after giving the First Impulse to Himself.

*The Father withdrew Himself, yet shut not up His own peculiar Fire within His Gnostic Power.*

K. 12.
C. 11.

"His own peculiar Fire" seems to mean

33

that which characterizes the One Mystery as Father, or creative. He withdrew Himself into Silence and Darkness, but left His Fire, or Fiery Mind, to operate the whole creation. May not this throw some light on the meaning of the obscure mystery-hymn at the end of the Christian Gnostic *Second Book of Ieou* (Carl Schmidt, *Gnost. Schrift.*, p. 187) ?

" I praise Thee . . .; for Thou hast drawn Thyself into Thyself altogether in Truth, till Thou hast set free the space of this Little Idea [? the manifested cosmos]; yet hast Thou not withdrawn Thyself."

## GOD-NURTURING SILENCE.

In the first passage from the Simonian *Great Announcement*, to which we have referred above (p. 31), the Great Power of the Father is called Incomprehensible Silence, and, as is well known, Silence (Sigē) was, in a number of systems of the Christianized Gnosis, the Syzygy, or Co-partner, or Complement, of the

Ineffable. Among the Pythagoræans and Trismegistic Gnostics also Silence was the condition of Wisdom.

Though there is no verse of our Oracle-poem preserved which sets this forth, there are phrases quoted by Proclus (K. 16) which speak of the Paternal Silence. It is the Divine "*Calm*," the "*Silence, Nurturer of the Divine*"; it is the unsurpassable unity of the Father, the that concerning which words fail; the mind must be silenced to know it—that is, to "*accord with*" it (K. 16, C. 12, 5).

Proclus in all probability had our Oracles in mind when he wrote (C. 12):

"For such is the Mind in that state, energizing prior to energizing [in the sensible world], in that it had in no way emanated, but rested in the Father's Depth [*i.e.*, its own Depth], and in the Sacred Shrine, held in the Arms of Silence, '*Nurturer of the Divine*.'"

Silence is known through mind alone. While things are objective to one, while

35

we are taught or told *about* things, they cannot be real. The Great Silence on the mind-side of things corresponds with the Great Sea on the matter-side of things; the latter is active, the former inactive; and the only way to attain wisdom, which is other than knowledge, is to "re-create" or re-generate oneself. Man only "knows" God by getting to this Silence, in which naught but the creative words of true Power are heard. He then no longer conceives formal ideas in his mind, but utters living ideas in all his acts—thoughts, words and deeds.

The Fatherhood is equated by Proclus (K. 13) with Essence (*ousía*), or Subsistence (*hyparxis*); the Motherhood with Life (*zōē*) or Power (*dynamis*); and the Sonship with Operation or Actuality (*enérgeia*). These philosophical terms are, of course, not the names used in the Oracles, which preferred more graphic, symbolic and poetical expressions.

36

## THE HOLY FIRE.

Thus Mind "in potentiality" is the "Hidden Fire" of Simon the Magian (who doubtless knew of the "Books of the Chaldæans"), and the "Manifested Fire" was the Mind "in operation" or Formative Mind. As *The Great Announcement* of the Simonian tradition has it (Hipp., *Ref.*, vi. 9-11):

"The hidden aspects of the Fire are concealed in the manifest, and the manifest produced in the hidden. . . .

"And the manifested side of the Fire has all things in itself which a man can perceive of things visible, or which he unconsciously fails to perceive ; whereas the hidden side is every thing which one can conceive as intelligible, or which a man fails to conceive."

And so in our Oracles, as with Simon, and with Heraclitus, who called it "Ever-living Fire," the greatest symbol of the Power of Deity was called "*Holy Fire*," as Proclus tells us (K. 13). This Fire was both intelligible and immaterial

37

and sensible and material, according to the point of view from which it was regarded.

MIND OF MIND.

The fiery self-creative Energy of the Father is regarded as intelligible ; that is, as determined by the vital potencies of Mind alone. Here all is " in potentiality " or hidden from the senses ; it is the truly " occult world." The sensible, or manifested, universe comes into existence by the demiurgic, or formative, or shaping Energy of the Mind, which now, as Architect of matter, is called Mind of Mind, or Mind Son of Mind, as we have Man Son of Man in the Christianized Chaldæan Gnosis. This is set forth in the following lines :

K. 13.
C. 22.

*For He [the Father] doth not in-lock His Fire transcendent, the Primal Fire, His Power, into Matter by means of works, but by energy of Mind. For it is Mind of Mind who is the Architect of this [the manifested] fiery world.*

38

"Works" seem here to mean activities, objects, creatures — separation. This Father, who is wholly beyond the Sea of Matter, does not shut up His Power into Matter by in-locking it in bodies, or works, or separate objects, but energizes by means of some mysterious abstract and infinite penetration—thus laying down as it were the foundations of root-form, the ground-plan so to speak, the nexus of the first Limit ; this makes Matter to assume the first beginnings of Mass. As soon as the Father, or Mind of all minds, has made this frame-work or net-work of Fire, Mind of Mind is born ; and this Mind is the Fiery Cosmic Mind, which by contacting Matter in its first essential nature generates the beginnings of the World-Body and of all bodies. This is the work of Mind of Mind.

So also we find the Supreme addressing Hermes in " The Virgin of the World " treatise as :

" Soul of My Soul, and Holy Mind of My own Mind " (*H.*, iii. 104).

And again in another Trismegistic fragment we read :

" There was One Gnostic Light alone— nay, Light transcending Gnostic Light. He is for ever Mind of Mind who makes that Light to shine " (*H.*, iii. 257).

For as our Oracles have it :

K. 14.
C. 13.

*The Father out-perfected all, and gave them over to His second Mind, whom ye, all nations of mankind, sing of as first.*

Intelligible Fire has the essence of all things for its " sparks " or " atoms." " Out-perfected " seems to mean that the Father of Himself is the Complement or Fulfilment of each separate thing. In a certain mystic sense, there are never more than two things in the universe—namely, any one thing which one may choose to think of, and its complement, the rest of the All ; and that completion of every imperfection is God.

The contention of the Gnostics was that the nations worshipped the Demiurgic or Fabricative Power of the Deity as His most transcendent mystery; this, they contended, was really a secondary mode of the Divine Power as compared with the mystery of the ineffable Self-determination of the Supreme.

A volume might be written on the subject, with innumerable quotations from Jewish and Christian Gnostics, from Philo and the Trismegistic writers, and from early Orientalist Platonists such as Numenius. The Father, as Absolute Mind, or Paramātman, perfects all things; but when we distinguish Spirit and Matter, when we regard the mystery from our state of duality, and imagine Matter as set over against Spirit, then the administration of Matter is said to be entrusted to Mind in operation in space and time; and this was called Mind of Mind, Mind Son of Mind, or Man Son of Man.

## THE MONAD AND DYAD.

This Mind of Mind is conceived as dual, as containing the idea of the Dyad, in contrast with the Paternal Mind which is the Monad—both terms of the Pythagoræan *mathēsis* or *gnōsis*. His duality consists in His having power over both the intelligible and sensible universe. This is set forth in our Oracles as follows :

K. 14.
C. 27.

*The Dyad hath His seat with Him [the Father] ; for He hath both—[both power] to master things intelligible [or ideal], and also to induce the sense of feeling in the world [of form].*

Nevertheless, there are not two Gods, but one ; not two Minds, but one ; not two Fires, but one ; for :

K. 15.
C. 13.

*All things have for their Father the One Fire.*

The Father is thus called the Paternal Monad.

K. 15.
C. 26.

*He is the all-embracing [lit., wide-stretching] Monad who begets the Two.*

## THE ONE BODY OF ALL THINGS.

In connection with this verse we may take the following two verses of very obscure reading :

*From both of these [the Monad and Dyad] there flows the Body of the Three, first yet not first ; for it is not by it that things intelligible are measured.*

This appears to mean that, for the sensible universe, the Body of the Triad —that is, the Mother-substance—comes first as being the container of all things sensible ; it is not, however, the measurer of things intelligible or ideal. It is first as Body, or the First or Primal Body, but Mind is prior to it.

## ONCE BEYOND AND TWICE BEYOND.

The Three Persons of the Supernal Triad were also called in the Oracles by the names Once Beyond, Twice Beyond and Hecatē ; when so called they seem to have been regarded by the

43

commentators as either simply synonyms
of the three Great Names, or else as in
some way the self-reflection of the Primal
Triad, or as the Primal Triad mirrored
in itself, that is in the One Body of all
things.

It is difficult to say what is the precise
meaning of the mystery-names Once
Beyond and Twice Beyond. If we take
them as designations of the self-reflected
Triad, it may be that Once Beyond was
so called because it was regarded as
Beyond, not in the sense of transcending,
but as beyond the threshold, so to say,
of the pure spiritual state, or, in other
words, as raying forth into manifestation ; and so also with Twice Beyond.
They paralleled the first and second
Minds of the Primal Unity.

Hecatē seems to have been the best
equivalent our Greek mystics could
find in the Hellenic pantheon for the
mysterious and awe - inspiring Primal
Mother or Great Mother of Oriental
mystagogy.

44

This reflected Trinity seems to have been regarded as the Three-in-one of the Second Mind. The Later Platonist commentators seem to have in general equated these names with their Kronos, Zeus and Rhea ; while an anonymous commentator earlier than Proclus tells us that Once Beyond is the Paternal Mind of all cosmic intellection ; Hecatē is the ineffable Power of this Mind and fills all things with intellectual light, but apparently does not enter them ; whereas Twice Beyond gives of himself into the worlds, and sows into them " *agile splendours,*" as the Oracles phrase it (K., 16, 17). All this is a refinement of intellectual subtlety that need not detain us ; it is foreign to the simpler mysticism of the Oracles.

THE GREAT MOTHER.

Hecatē is the Great Mother or Life of the universe, the Magna Mater, or Mother of the Gods and all creatures.

She is the Spouse of Mind, and

D                45

simultaneously Mother and Spouse of Mind of Mind ; she is, therefore, said to be centered between them.

K. 27.
C. 65.

*'Mid the Fathers the Centre of Hecatē circles.*

She is the Mother of souls, the In-breather of life. Concerning this cosmic " vitalizing," or " quickening," or " en-souling" (*psychōsis*), as Proclus calls it, three obscure verses are preserved :

K. 28.
C. 38.

*About the hollows beneath the ribs of her right side there spouts, full-bursting, forth the Fountain of the Primal Soul, all at once ensouling Light, Fire, Æther, Worlds.*

If the " hollows beneath the ribs " is the correct translation (for the Greek seems very faulty, no matter what license we give to poetic imagery), it would appear that Hecatē, the Great Mother, or World-Soul, was figured in woman's form. Hecatē is, of course, as

46

we have already remarked, not her native name (*nomen barbarum*), but the best equivalent the Greeks could find in their humanized pantheon, a *bourgeois* company as compared with the majestic, awesome and mysterious divinities of the Orient.

This was the cosmic *psychōsis*; the mixture of individual souls was—according to the Trismegistic "Virgin of the World" treatise, and as we might naturally expect—of a somewhat more substantial, or plastic, nature. In this treatise we read:

"And since it neither thawed when fire was set to it (for it was made of Fire), nor yet did freeze when it had once been properly produced (for it was made of Breath), but kept its mixture's composition a certain special kind, peculiar to itself, of special type and special blend—(which composition you must know, God called *psychōsis* . . .)—it was from this coagulate He fashioned souls enough in myriads" (*H.*, iii. 99).

47

It was probably in the mouth of the Great Mother that our poet placed the following lines :

K. 28.
C. 18.

*After the Father's Thinkings, you must know, I, the Soul, dwell, making all things to live by Heat.*

In the mystery of re-generation also, as soon as the conception from the Father takes place—the implanting of the Light-spark, or germ of the spiritual man—the soul of the man becomes sensible to the passion of the Great Soul, the One and Only Soul, and he feels himself pulsing in the fiery net-work of lives.

But why, it may be asked, does the great Life-stream come forth from the Mother's right side ? The fragments we possess do not tell us ; but the original presumably contained some description of the Mother-Body, for we are told :

*On the left side of Hecatē is a Fountain*   K. 28.
*of Virtue, remaining entirely within, not*   C. 187.
*sending forth its pure virginity.*

We have thus to think out the symbolism in a far more vital mode than the figurative expressions naturally suggest. And again :

*And from her back, on either side the*   K. 29.
*Goddess, boundless Nature hangs.*   C. 141.

This suggests that Nature is the Garment or Mantle of the Goddess-Mother. The Byzantine commentators ascribe to every Limb of the Mother the power of life-giving ; every Limb and Organ was a fountain of life. Her hair, her temples, the top of her head, her sides or flanks, were all so regarded ; and even her dress, the coverings or veilings of her head, and her girdle. Whether they had full authority for this in the original text we do not know. Kroll considers this " *fraus aperta* " (K. 29) ; but the Mother of Life

49

must be All-Life, one would have naturally thought, and one verse still preserved to us reads :

K. 29.
C. 128.

*Her hair seems like a Mane of Light a-bristle piercingly.*

Damascius speaks of her crown ; this may possibly have been figured as the wall-crown or turreted diadem of Cybelē (Rhea), in which case it might have typified the " Walls of Fire " of Stoic tradition.

Her girdle seems to have been figured as a serpent of fire.

The Great Mother is also called Rhea in the Oracles, as the following three verses inform us :

K. 30.
C. 59.

*Rhea, in sooth, is both the Fountain and the Flood of the blest Knowing Ones ; for she it is who first receives the Father's Powers into her countless Bosoms, and poureth forth on every thing birth [-and-death] that spins like to a wheel.*

The " Knowing Ones " are the Intel- ligences or Gnostic Thoughts of the Father. She is the Mother of Genesis, the Wheel or Sphere of Re-becoming. In one of her aspects she is called in the Oracles the "*wondrous and awe-inspiring Goddess*," as Proclus tells us. With the above verses may be compared K. 36, C. 140, 125 below.

## ALL THINGS ARE TRIPLE.

The statement of Hippolytus that the Assyrians (*i.e.*, the Chaldæans) " were the first to consider the soul triple and yet one," is borne out by several quotations from our Oracle-poem.

*The Mind of the Father uttered [the Word] that all should be divided [or cut] into three. His Will nodded assent, and at once all things were so divided.*

K. 18.
C. 28.

The Father-Mind thought " Three," acted " Three." Thought and action agreed, and it immediately happened.

51

An apparent continuation of this is found in the lines which characterize the Forth-thinker as :

K. 18.
C. 29.

*He who governs all things with the Mind of the Eternal.*

This fundamental Triplicity of all things is "intelligible," that is to say, determined by the Mind. The Mind is the Great Measurer, Divider and Separator. Thus Philo of Alexandria writes concerning the Logos, or Mind or Reason of God :
"So God, having sharpened His Reason (Logos), the Divider of all things, cut off both the formless and undifferentiated essence of all things, and the four elements of cosmos which had been separated out of it [*sci*., the essence, or quintessence], and the animals and plants which had been compacted by means of these" (*H*., i. 236).

We learn from Damascius also that, according to our Oracles, the "ideal division" (? of all things into three) was the "*root (or source) of every division*" in the sensible universe (K. 18, C. 58). This law was summed up as follows :

*In every cosmos there shineth [or is manifested] a Triad, of which a Monad is source.*  K. 18.
C. 36.

It is this Triad that "*measures and delimits all things*" (K. 18, C. 8) from highest to lowest. And again :

*All things are served in the Gulphs of the Triad.*  K. 18.
C. 31.

This is very obscure; but perhaps the following verse may throw some light on the imagery :

*From this Triad the Father mixed every spirit.*  K. 18.
C. 30.

In the first verse "Gulphs" are generally translated by "Bosoms," and "are served" by "are governed"; but

53

the latter expression is a technical Homeric term for serving the wine for libation purposes from the great mixing-bowl (*kratēr*) into the cups, and the mixing, or mingling or blending, of souls is operated, in Plato, in the great Mixing-bowl of the Creator. These gulphs are thus mother-vortices in primal space.

The " Three " is the number of determination, and therefore stands for the root-conditioning of form, and of all classification. But if the " Three " from one point of view is formative, and therefore determining and limiting, from another point of view, it endows with power ; and so one of our Oracles runs :

*K.* 51.
*C.* 170.
*Arming both mind and soul with triple Might.*

In the original, "triple" is a poetical term that might be rendered " three-barbed "; if, however, it is to be connected with Pythagoræan nomenclature, it would denote a triple angle—that is

54

to say, presumably, the solid angle of a tetrahedron or regular four-faced pyramid.

## THE MOTHER-DEPTHS.

The Bosoms or Gulphs (? Vortices, Voragines, Whirl-swirls, Æons, Atoms) are also called Depths—a technical term of very frequent occurrence in all the Gnostic schools of the time. The Great Depth of all depths was that of the Father, the Paternal Depth. Thus one of our Oracles reads

*Ye who, understanding, know the Paternal Depth cosmos-transcending.*

K. 18.
C. 168.

This Paternal Depth is the ultimate mystery ; but from another point of view it may be regarded as the Intelligible Ordering of all things. It is called super-cosmic or cosmos-transcending, when cosmos is regarded as the sensible or manifested order; it is the Occult, or Hidden, Eternal Type of universals, or wholes, simultaneously interpenetrating one another, undivided (sensibly) yet divided (intelligibly). We are told, therefore, concerning this super-cosmic or trans-mundane Depth, that

K. 19.    *It is all things, but intelligibly [all].*

That is to say, in it things are not divided in time and space ; there is no sensible separation. It is not the specific state, or state of species ; but the state of wholes or genera. It is neither Father nor Mother, yet both. It is the state of " At Once " ; and perhaps this may explain the strange term " Once Beyond " —that is, the At-Once in the state of the Beyond, beyond the sensible divided cosmos. Proclus and Damascius speak of it as " of the form of oneness " and " indivisible " ; and an Oracle characterizes it as :

K. 19.    *That which cannot be cut up ; the Holder-together of all sources.*

As such it may be regarded as the Mother-side of things, and thus is called :

*Source of [all] sources, Womb that holds all things together.*    K. 19.
C. 99.

The Later Platonic commentators compared this with Plato's *Auto-zōon*, the Living Thing-in-itself, the Source of life to all ; and thus the That-which-gives-life-to-itself ; and, therefore, the Womb of all living creatures. The Oracles, however, regard it as the Womb of Life, the Divine Mother.

*She is the Energizer* [lit., *Work-woman*]    K. 19.
*and Forth-giver of Life-bringing Fire.*    C. 55.

"She fills the Life-giving Bosom [or Womb] of Hecatē." — the Supernal Mother's self-reflection in the sensible universe—says Proclus, basing himself on an Oracle, and :

*Flows fresh and fresh* [or *on and on*]    K. 19.
*into the wombs of things.*    C. 55.

57

The " wombs of things " are, literally, the " holders-together of things." They are reflections of the Great " Holder-together of all sources " of the fourth fragment back. This poetical expression for the Mother-Depth and her infinite reflections in her own nature of manifoldness, was developed by the Later Platonic commentators into the formal designation of a hierarchy—the Synoches. That which she imparts is called :

K. 19.     *The Life-giving Might of Fire possessed of mighty power.*

This is all on the Mother-side of things ; but this should never be divorced from the Father-side, as may be seen from the nature of the mysterious Æon.

THE ÆON.

On the æon-doctrine (*cf. H.*, i. 387-412), which probably occupied a prominent position in the mysticism of our Oracle-poem (though, of course, in a

58

simple form and not as in the over- developed æonology of the Christianized Gnosis), we unfortunately possess only four verses.

One of the names given to the Æon was "*Father-begotten*" Light, because "He makes to shine His unifying light on all," as Proclus tells us.

*For He [the Æon] alone, culling unto its full the Flower of Mind [the Son] from out the Father's Might [the Mother], possesseth [both] the power to understand the Father's Mind, and to bestow that Mind both on all sources and upon all principles,—both power to understand [al., whirl], and ever bide upon His never-tiring pivot.*

K. 27.
C. 71.

The nature of this Æonic Principle (or Ātmic Mystery), according to the belief of the Theurgists, is described by Proclus. But whether this description was based upon our poem or not, we cannot be certain. We, therefore, append what Proclus says, in illustration only (C. 2) :

" Theurgists declare that He [Duration, Time without bounds, the Æon] is God, and hymn His divinity as both older [than old], and younger [than young], as ever-circling into itself [the Egg] and æon-wise ; both as conceiving the sum total of all numbered things that move within the cosmos of His Mind, yet, over and beyond them all, as infinite by reason of His Power, and yet [again, when] viewed with them, as spirally convolved [the Serpent]."

The " ever-circling " is the principle of self-motivity. On the spiral-side of things there is procession to infinity ; while on the sphere-side beginning and end are immediate and " at once."

With this passage must be taken two others quoted by Taylor, but without giving the references (C. 3 and 4) :   .

" God [energizing] in the cosmos, æon-ian, boundless, young and old, in spiral mode convolved."

60

"For Eternity [the Æon], according to the Oracles, is Cause of Life that never falleth short, and of untiring Power, and restless Energy."

THE UTTERANCE OF THE FIRE.

In connection with the idea of the Living Intellectual Fire as the Perfect Intelligible, Father and Mother in one (both creating Matter and impregnating it), conceived of sensibly as the "Descent into Matter," we may, perhaps, take the following verses :

*Thence there leaps forth the Genesis of* K. 20.
*Matter manifoldly wrought in varied* C. 101.
*colours. Thence the Fire-flash down-stream-* 24.
*ing dims its [fair] Flower of Fire, as it*
*leaps forth into the wombs of worlds.*
*For thence all things begin downwards*
*to shoot their admirable rays.*

The origin of matter and the genesis of matter is thus to be sought for in the Intelligible itself. The doctrine of the

Pythagoræans and Platonists was that the origin of matter was to be traced to the Monad. The Flower of Fire is here the quintessence of it.

LIMIT THE SEPARATOR.

To the same part of the poem we must also refer the following :

K. 20.
C. 66.

*For from Him leap forth both Thunderings inexorable, and the Fireflash-receiving Bosoms of the All-fiery Radiance of Father-begotten Hecatē, and that by which the Flower of Fire and mighty Breath beyond the fiery poles is girt.*

Those who have studied attentively the *Mithriac Ritual* (Vol. VI.), will feel themselves in a familiar atmosphere when reading these lines. The " Thunderings " are the Creative Utterances of the Father ; the " Bosoms " of Hecatē are the receptive vortices on the Mother-side of things. Yet Father and Mother and also Son are all three the Monad. She is " Father-begotten," and He the Son is Mother-begotten—the Monad perpetually giving birth to itself. The Son is the that which " girds " or limits or separates, the Gnostic Horos or Limit, the Form-side of things, which shuts out the Below from the Above, and determines all opposites. It is the Cross, the " Undergirding " of the universe, as we have seen in *The Gnostic Crucifixion* (Vol. VII., pp. 15, 43 ff.).

The commentators, however, with their rage for intellectual precision, have turned this into a technical term, making it a special name ; but in the Oracles *Hypezōkós* is used more simply and generally as the separator.

Proclus characterizes this Hypezōkós as the prototype of division, the " separation of the things-that-are from matter," basing himself apparently on the verse :

*Just as a diaphragm* [hypezōkós], *a*    K. 22. *knowing membrane, He divides.*

63

The nature of this separation is that of " knowing " or " gnostic " Fire. The Epicuræans called the separation between the visible and invisible the " Flaming Walls " of the universe. Compare the Angel with the flaming sword who guards the Gates of Paradise.

So also with the epithet " inexorable " (*ameíliktoi*) applied to the "Thunderings"; these have been transformed by the over-elaboration of the commentators into a hierarchy of Inexorables or Implacables, just as is the gorgeous imagery of the Coptic Gnostic treatises of the Askew and Bruce codices.

The simpler use may be seen in the following two verses :

K. 21.    *The Mind of the Father, vehicled in*
C. 17.  *rare Drawers-of-straight-lines, flashing inflexibly in furrows of implacable Fire.*

This seems to refer to the Rays of the Divine Intelligence vehicled in creative

64

Fire. It is the Divine Ploughing of primal substance. Straight lines are characteristic of the Mind.

It is the first furrowing, so to speak, of the Sea of Matter in a universal pattern that impresses upon the surface a network of Light (as may be seen in protoplasm under a strong microscope) from the Ruler of the Sea above. It is the first Descent of the Father, and the first Ascent or Arising of the Son; it suggests the idea of riding and controlling. The epithet "rare" or "attenuated" suggests drawn out to the finest thread; these threads or lines govern and map out the Sea; they are the Lines on the Surface; they glitter and look like furrows of the essence of Fire.

## THE EMANATION OF IDEAS.

In close connection with the lines beginning "For from Him leap forth," we may take the longest fragment (16 lines) preserved to us:

65

*The Father's Mind forth-bubbled, conceiving, with His Will in all its prime, Ideas that can take upon themselves all forms; and from One Source they, taking flight, sprang forth. For from the Father was both Will and End.*

*These were made differentiate by Gnostic Fire, allotted into different knowing modes.*

*For, for the world of many forms, the King laid out an intellectual Plan [or Type] not subject unto change. Kept to the tracing of this Plan, that no world can express, the World, made glad with the Ideas that take all shapes, grew manifest with form.*

*Of these Ideas there is One only Source, from which there bubble-forth in differentiation other [ones] that no one can approach—forth-bursting round the bodies of the World—which circle round its awe-inspiring Depths [or Bosoms], like unto swarms of bees, flashing around them and about, incuriously, some hither and some thither,—the Gnostic Thoughts from the Paternal Source that cull unto their full*

66

*the Flower of Fire at height of sleepless Time.*

*It was the Father's first self-perfect Source that welled-forth these original Ideas.*

With this " culling " or " plucking " of the Flower of Fire compare the ancient gnomic couplet preserved by Hesiod (*O. et D.*, 741 f.) :
" Nor from Five-branched at Gods' Fire-
    looming
   Cut Dry from Green with flashing
    Blade."
As has been previously stated (*H.*, i. 265, n. 5), I believe that Hesiod has preserved this scrap of ancient wisdom from the " Orphic " fragments in circulation in his day among the people in Bœotia, who had them from an older Greece than that of Homer's heroes ; in other words, that we have in it a trace of the contact of pre-Homeric Greece with " Chaldæa."

These living Ideas or creative Thoughts are emanations (or forth-flowings) of the Divine Mind, and constitute the Plan

67

of that Mind, the Divine Economy. They are more transcendent even than the Fire, for they are said to be able to gather for themselves the subtlest essence or Flower of Fire. "At height of sleepless Time " is a beautiful phrase, though it is difficult to assign to it a very precise meaning. The " height of Time " is, perhaps, the supreme moment, and thus may mean momentarily—not, however, in the sense of lasting only the smallest fraction of time, but referring to Time at its limit where it touches Eternity.

The Thoughts of the Father-Mind are on the Borderland of Time. They are living Intelligences of Light and Life, of the nature of Logoi.

*K.* 24.  *Thoughts of the Father! Brightness a-flame, pure Fire!*

THE BOND OF LOVE DIVINE.

Next we may take the verses referring to the Birth of Love (Erōs), the Bond-of-union between all things.

68

*For the Self-begotten One, the Father-* K. 25.
*Mind, perceiving His [own] Works, sowed* C. 107.
*into all Love's Bond, that with his Fire*
*o'ermasters all ; so that all might continue*
*loving on for endless time, and that these*
*Weavings of the Father's Gnostic Light*
*might never fail. With this Love, too, it is*
*the Elements of Cosmos keep on running.*

The Works of the Father are the
Operations of the Divine Mind—the Souls.
The same idea, though on a lower scale,
so to say, may be seen in the Announcement of the Monarch of the Worlds,
sitting on the Throne of Truth, to the
Souls, in the Trismegistic "Virgin of
the World " treatise :

" O Souls, Love and Necessity shall be
your Lords, they who are Lords and
Marshals after Me of all " (*H.*, ii. 110).

The Marriage of the Elements and their
perpetual transmutation was one of the
leading doctrines of Heraclitus. The
Elements married and transformed themselves into one another, as may also be

seen from the Magian myth quoted in Vol. V. of these little books, *The Mysteries of Mithra* (pp. 49-52). The idea is summed up in the following fine lines from a Hymn of Praise to the Æon or Eternity, in the Magic Papyri :

" Hail unto Thee, O Thou Beginning and Thou End of Nature naught can move ! Hail unto Thee, Thou Vortex of the Liturgy [or Service] unweariable of Nature's Elements ! "

In close connection with the above verses of our poem we must plainly take the following :

K. 25.
C. 23.

*With the Bond of admirable Love, who leaped forth first, clothed round with Fire, his fellow bound to him, that he might mix the Mixing-bowls original by pouring in the Flower of his own Fire.*

In the last line I read ἐπιχῶν (" pouring in ") for ἐπισχών. The Mixing-bowls, or Kratēres, are the Fiery Crucibles in which the elements and souls of things are mixed. The Mixer is not Love as apart from the Father, but the Mind of the Father as Love, as we learn from the following verses :

*Having mingled the Spark of Soul with*    K. 26.
*two in unanimity—with Mind and Breath*    C. 81.
*Divine—to them He added, as a third,*
*pure Love, the august Master binding all.*

Compare with this the Mixing of Souls in " The Virgin of the World " treatise :
" For taking breath from His own Breath and blending with it Knowing Fire, He mingled them with other substances which have no power to know ; and having made the two—either with other—one, with certain hidden Words of Power, He thus set all the mixture going thoroughly " (*H.*, iii. 98).
This Chaste and Holy and Divine Love is invoked as follows in the Paris Papyrus (1748) :
" Thee I invoke, Thou Primal Author of all generation, who dost out-stretch

71

Thy wings o'er all the universe; Thee the unapproachable, Thee the immeasurable, who dost inspire into all souls the generative sense [*lit.*, reason], who dost conjoin all things by power of Thine own Self " (K. 26).

Elsewhere in the same Papyrus (1762), Love is called :

" The Hidden One who secretly doth cause to spread among all souls the Fire that cannot be attained by contemplation."

What men think of as love, is, as contrasted with this Divine Love, called in our Oracles, the " *stifling of True Love.*" True Love is also called " *Deep Love,*" with which we are to fill our souls, as Proclus tells us (K. 26). Elsewhere in the Oracles this Love was united with Faith and Truth into a triad, which may be compared with another triad in the following verse quoted by Damascius :

K. 27.  *Virtue and Wisdom and deliberate Cer-*
C. 35.  *tainty.*

So far we have been dealing with the Divine Powers when conceived as transcending the manifested universe; we now come to the world-shaping, or economy of the material cosmos, and to the Powers concerned with it.

## THE SEVEN FIRMAMENTS.

As we have seen above, in treating of the Great Mother (p. 46), it is she who, as the Primal Soul, "all at once ensouls Light, Fire, Æther, Worlds" (K. 28, C. 38).

The Later Platonist commentators regard this Light as a monad embracing a triad of states—empyrean, ætherial, and hylic (that is, of gross matter). They further assert that the last state only is visible to normal physical sight (K. 31).

73

These four thus constituted the quaternary or tetrad of the whole sensible universe. This would, of course, be somewhat of a daring " philosophizing " of the simple statement of the original poem, if the verse we have quoted were the only authority for the precise statement of the commentators. But we are hardly justified in assuming, as Kroll appears to do throughout, that if no verse is quoted, therefore no verse existed. The Platonic commentators had the full poem before them, and (like the systematizers of the Upaniṣhads) tried to evolve a consistent system out of its mystic utterances. There were also, in the highest probability, other Hellenistic documents of a similar character, giving back some reflections from the " Books of the Chaldæans " ; and also in the air a kind of general tradition of a " Chaldæan philosophy."

The Sensible Universe was thus divided by them, basing themselves on the pregnant imagery of the Oracles, into three states or "planes" — the empyrean, ætherial, and hylic. To these planes or states they referred the mysterious septenary of spheres mentioned in the verse :

*The Father caused to swell forth seven firmaments of worlds.*    K. 31. C. 120.

This Father is, of course, Mind of Mind, and the "causing to swell forth" gives the idea of the swelling from a centre to the limit of a surround.

The most interesting point is that those who knew the Oracles, and were in the direct line of their tradition, did not regard these seven firmaments or zones as the "planetary orbits." One of the seven they assigned to the empyrean, three to the ætherial, and three to the gross-material or sublunary. There was thus a chain or coil of seven depending from the eighth, the octave, of Light, the Borderland between the intelligible and the sensible worlds. All the seven,

75

however, were "corporeal" worlds (K. 32). The three hylic (those of gross matter) may be compared with the solid, liquid and gaseous states of physical matter; the three ætherial with similar states of æther or subtle matter; and the seventh corresponds with the atomic or empyrean or true fiery or fire-mist state.

Moreover, as to the hylic world or world of gross matter, which had three spheres or states, we learn:

K. 33.     *The centres of the hylic world are fixed in the æther above it.*

That is to say, presumably, the æther was supposed to surround and interpenetrate the cosmos of gross matter.

THE TRUE SUN.

As to the Sun, the tradition handed on a mysterious doctrine that cannot now be completely recovered in the absence of the original text. Proclus, however, tells us that the real Sun, as distinguished from the visible disk, was trans-mundane or super-cosmic—that is, beyond the worlds visible to the senses. In other words, it belonged to the Light-world proper, the monadic cosmos, and poured forth thence its "fountains of Light." The tradition of the most arcane or mystic of the Oracles, he tells us, was that the Sun's "wholeness"—*i.e.*, monad —was to be sought on the trans-mundane plane (K. 32, C. 130); "for there," he says, "is the '*Solar Cosmos*' and the '*Whole Light*,' as the Oracles of the Chaldæans say, and I believe " (K 33).

Elsewhere he speaks of "what appears to be the circuit of the Sun," and contrasts this with its true circulation, "which, proceeding from above somewhence, from out the hidden and super-celestial ordering of things beyond the heavens, sows into all the [suns] in cosmos the proper portion of their light for each." This also seems to have been based on the doctrine of the Oracles.

As the Enforming Mind was called Mind of Mind, so was the "truer Sun" called in the Oracles "*Time of Time*," because it measures all things with Time, as Proclus tells us; and this Time is, of course, the Æon. It was also called "*Fire, Sluice of Fire*," and also "*Fire-disposer*" (K. 33, C. 133), and, we may add, by many another name connected with Fire, as we learn from the *Mithriac Ritual*.

## THE MOON.

If the visible sun, as we have seen, was not the true Sun, equally so must we suppose the visible moon to be an image of the true Moon reflected in the atmosphere of gross matter. Concerning the Moon we have these five scattered shreds of fragments.

K. 33.
C. 135.

*Both the ætherial course and the measure-less rush and the aërial floods* [or *fluxes*] *of the Moon.*

*O Æther, Sun, Moon's Breath, Leaders of Air!*    K. 33.
C. 136.

*Both of the solar circles and lunar pulsings and aërial bosoms.*    K. 33.
C. 139.

*The melody of Æther and of Sun, and of the streams of Moon and Air.*    K. 33.
C. 139.

*And wide Air, and lunar course, and the ætherial vault of Sun.*    K. 34.
C. 137.

These scraps are too fragmentary to comment on with much profit.


**THE ELEMENTS.**

From what remains we learn, as Proclus tells us, that the Sun-space came first, then the Moon-space, and then the Air-space. The Elements of cosmos, however, were not simply our Earthy fire, air, water, and earth, but of a greater order. Thus Olympiodorus tells us that the elements at the highest points

79

of the earth, that is on the tops of the highest mountains, were also thought of as elements of cosmic Water—as it were Watery air ; and this air in its turn was (? moist) Æther, while Æther itself was the uttermost Æther ; it was in that state that were to be sought the "*Æthers of the Elements*" proper, as the Oracles call them (K. 34, C. 112).

## THE SHELLS OF THE COSMIC EGG.

The diagrammatic representation of cosmic limit was a curve ; whether hyperbolic, parabolic or elliptical we do not know. Damascius, quoting from the Oracles, speaks of it as a single line— "*drawn out in a curved (or convex) outline,*" or figure ; and adds that this figure was frequently used in the Oracles (K. 34). It signified the periphery of heaven.

In the Orphic mythology (doubtless based on " Chaldæan " sources) the dome of heaven is fabled to have been formed out of the upper shell of the Great Egg, when it broke in twain. The Egg in its upper half was sphere-like, in its lower "conical" or elliptical.

Proclus tells us that the Oracles taught that there were seven circuits or rounds of the irregular or imperfect "spheres," and in addition the single motion of the eighth or perfect sphere which carried the whole heaven round in the contrary direction towards the west.

## THE PHYSIOLOGY OF THE COSMIC BODY.

To this eighth sphere we must refer the " progression," spoken of in the verses :

*Both lunar course and star-progression.* K. 34.
*[This] star-progression was not delivered* C. 144.
*from the womb of things because of thee.*

Man, the normal mind of man, was subject to the irregular spheres ; he is egg-shaped and not spherical. And if there were spheres there were also certain mysterious " centres," and " channels " —pipes, canals, conduits, or ducts ; but

81

what and how many these were, we can no longer discover owing to the loss of the original text. One obscure fragment alone remains :

K. 35.
C. 92.

*And fifth, [and] in the midst, another fiery sluice, whence the life-bringing Fire descendeth to the hylic channels.*

This apparently concerns the anatomy and physiology of the Great Body. Proclus introduces this quotation with the statement : " The conduit of the Power-of-generating-lives descends into the centre [of the cosmos], as also the Oracles say, when discoursing on the middle one of the five centres that extends right through to the opposite [side], through the centre of the earth."

How a centre can enter and go through another centre is not clear. These channels or centres, however, were clearly ways of conveying the nourishing and sustaining Fire to the world and all the lives in it.

The Primal Centre of the universe is presumably referred to in the following verse :

*The Centre, from which all [? rays] to the periphery are equal.*  K. 65. C. 124.

## THE GLOBULAR COSMOS.

In any case the root-plan of the universe was globular. Proclus tells us that God as the Demiurge, or World-shaper, made the whole cosmos :

*From Fire, from Water, Earth, and all-nourishing Æther.*  K. 35. C. 118.

Where Æther is presumably the " Watery Æther " or Air, as we have seen above (p. 80). He tells us further that the Maker, working by Himself, or on Himself, or with His own Hands, framed, or shaped (*lit.*, " carpentered ") the cosmos, as follows :

*Yea, for there was a Second Mass of Fire working of its own self all things*  K. 35. C. 108.

*below* (lit., *there*), *in order that the Cosmic Body might be wound into a ball, in order that Cosmos might be made plainly manifest, and not appear as membrane-like.*

It is, of course, very difficult to guess the meaning of these scraps without their context. The appearance of cosmos as membranous, however, suggests the idea of the thinnest skin or surface, that is the lines, or threads, or initial markings, on the surface of things ; that is to say, that the action of the Enforming Fire rolls up the surfaces of things into three-dimensional things or solids (even as the threads of wool are wound into a ball). The underlying idea may be seen in another Oracle, which, referring to the Path of Return, where the mode of Outgoing, or Involving, has to be reversed or unwound, warns us :

*K.* 64.
*C.* 152.

*Do not soil the spirit, nor turn the plane into the solid.*

To this we shall return later on at the end of our comments. (*Cf. H.*, iii. 174).

The "Second Mass of Fire" is, presumably, the Sensible Fire, or rather the Fire that brings into manifestation the sensible world, as contrasted with the Pure Hidden Fire—the Unmanifest, Intelligible or Ideal Mind of the Father. The Second is of course Mind of Mind, poetically figured, as contrasted with Mind in itself; it is Mind going forth from itself.

The word translated "Mass" ($\ddot{o}\gamma\kappa o\varsigma$) has a variety of refined meanings in Greek philosophical language; it can mean space, dimension, atom, etc., and gives the idea of the simplest determination of Body.

The World or Cosmos is, so to say, the "Outline" of the Mind turned to the thought of Body:

*For it is a Copy of Mind; but that which is brought forth* [or *engendered*] *has something of Body.*

K. 35.
C. 110.

85

NATURE AND NECESSITY.

The whole of Nature, of growth and evolution, depends, or derives its origin, from the Great Mother, the Spouse of Deity, as we have seen from the verse quoted above (p. 49, K. 29, C. 141). In some way Nature is identified with Fate and Custom, as the following three verses show : ..

K. 36.
C. 140.
125.

*For Nature that doth never tire, rules over worlds and works ; in order that the Heaven may run its course for aye, down-drawn, and the swift Sun, around its Centre, that custom-wise he may return.*

If by Apollo Proclus means the Sun, and if " one of the Theurgists " is a reference to the writer of our poem, then the words " *exulting in the Harmony of Light* " may be compared with the familiar " rejoicing as a giant to run his course." The Oracles speak of the Sun as possessing " *three-powered* (lit., *three-*

86

*winged*) *rule* "—that is, presumably, above, on, and beneath the earth.

## THE PRINCIPLES OR RULERS OF THE SENSIBLE WORLD.

In the fragments that remain it is very rare to find the Powers that administer the government of the universe, given Greek names. Though Proclus refers the following verse to Athēna, there is nothing to show that her name was mentioned in the Oracles. It is more probable (as we may see from K. 51, C. 170, below) that the phrase refers to the soul, or rather the new-born man of gnostic power, who leaps forth from his lower nature. Proclus may have seen in this an analogy with the birth of Athēna full-armed from the head of Zeus, and so the confusion has arisen. The phrase runs :

*Yea, verily, full-armed within and armed without, like to a goddess.*

K. 36.
C. 171.

The first epithet is used of the Trojan Horse with the armed warriors within it. In the mystery of re-generation this may refer to the re-making of all man's " bodies " according to the cut and pattern of the Great or Cosmic Body. This would be all on the Mother-side of things— the gestation of the true Body of Resurrection.

It is the Later Platonic commentators, most probably, who have added names from the Hellenic pantheon in elaborating the simple, and for the most part nameless, statements of the original poem.

It is, however, clear that corresponding with what are called Fountains ($\pi\eta\gamma\alpha\iota$) when considered as Sources of Light and Life, in the Intelligible, there were Principles, Rulerships or Sovereignties ($\dot{\alpha}\rho\chi\alpha\iota$), which ruled and ordered the Sensible Cosmos.

That these were divided into a hierarchy of four triads, twelve in all, as our commentators would have it, matches,

it is true, with the Twelve of the tradi-
tional Chaldæan star-lore ; but this was
probably not so definitely set forth in
the original text.  Concerning these Principles the following lines are preserved :

*Principles which, perceiving in their*
*minds the Works thought in the Father's*
*Mind, clothed them about with works and*
*bodies that the sense can apprehend.*

K. 37.
C. 73.

The chief ruling Principles of the
sensible world were three in number.
Damascius calls them " the three
Fathers "—*sci.*, of the manifested cosmos ;
but this seems to be an echo of the
nomenclature of the Theurgic or Magical
school and not of the Oracles proper.
He, however, quotes the following three
verses with regard to the threefold
division of the sensible world.

*Among them the first Course is the*
*Sacred one ; and in the midst the Aëry ;*
*third is another [one] which warms the*

K. 37.
C. 37.

89

*Earth in Fire. For all things are the slaves of these three mighty Principles.*

This seems to mean, according to Damascius, that corresponding with the Heaven, Earth, and the Interspace, Air, there are three Principles; or rather, there is One Principle in three modes—heavenly (or empyrean), middle (aëry or ætherial), and terrene (or hylic). The heavenly course is, presumably, the revolution of the Great Sphere of fixed stars; the terrene is connected with the Central Fire; and the middle with the motions of the irregular spheres.

It may also be that the last "course," connected with the Air simply, has to do with the mysterious "Winds" or currents of the Great Breath, as we saw in the symbolism of the *Mithriac Ritual*. This conjecture is confirmed by certain obscure references in Damascius, when, using the language of the Oracles, he speaks of a *" Pipe "* or *" Conduit "* connected with the Principles of the sensible world, and says that this is sub- ordinate to a Pipe connected with the Fountains of the intelligible world.

The difference between Fountain and Principle is clear enough ; one wells out from itself, the other rules something not itself. The terms seem to be somewhat of a *hysteron proteron* if we insist on a precise meaning ; we should remember, however, that we are dealing largely with symbolism and poetical imagery.

Proclus endeavours to draw up a precise scale of terms in connection with this imagery of Fountains or Sources, when he tells us that the highest point of every chain (or series) is called a Fountain (or Source) ; next came Springs ; after these Channels ; and then Streams. But this is probably a refinement of Proclus' and not native to the Logia.

# THE CHALDÆAN ORACLES.

## VOLUME II.

## CONTENTS.

---

## BIBLIOGRAPHY.

*K.* = Kroll (G.), *De Oraculis Chaldaicis;* in *Breslauer philologische Abhandlungen*, Bd. vii., Hft. i. (Breslau ; 1894).

*C.* = Cory (I. P.), *Ancient Fragments* (London ; 2nd ed., 1832), pp. 239—280. The first and third editions do not contain the text of our Oracles.

*F.* = Mead (G. R. S.), *Fragments of a Faith Forgotten* (London ; 2nd. ed.; 1906).

*H.* = Mead (G. R. S.), *Thrice Greatest Hermes* (London ; 1906).

# THE CHALDÆAN ORACLES.

## FRAGMENTS AND COMMENTS.

*(Continued.)*

## THE STARTERS.

On the borderland between the intelligible and sensible worlds were the Iynges—mysterious beings whose name may perhaps be translated as Wheels or Whirls, or even as Shriekers. As, however, I seem to detect in these three ruling Principles a correspondence with the creators, preservers and destroyers, or rather regenerators (perfecters or enders) of Indian theosophy, I will call these Iynges Starters, in the sense of Initiators or Setters-up of the initial impulse.

We will first set down the "wisdom" of the lexicon on this puzzling subject, warning the reader that he is having his attention turned to the wrong side of the thing—the littleness and superstition of what in the Oracles was clearly intended to be a revelation of some greatness.

*Iynx* is said to be the bird which we call the wryneck; it was called *iynx* in Greek from its cry, as it is called wryneck in English from the movement of its head. *Iygē* and *iygmós* are used of howling, shrieking, yelling, both for shouts of joy and cries of pain, and also of the hissing of snakes.

The ancient wizards, it is said, used to bind the wryneck to a wheel, which they made to revolve, in the belief that they thus drew men's hearts along with it and chained them to obedience; hence this magic wheel was frequently used in the belief that it was a means of recovering unfaithful lovers. This operation was called setting the magic bird or magic wheel agoing. The unfortunate bird seems to have been attached to the wheel with its wings and legs pegged

10

out crosswise so as to form four spokes, spread-eagle fashion. The word *iynx* thus came to mean a charm, and a spell, and also a passionate yearning.

The root-idea accordingly seems to have been that of a " winged wheel " that emitted sound, and we are reminded of the winged creatures or wheels in the famous Vision of Ezekiel, who saw the mystic sight in Babylon, and thus probably caught some reflection of the symbolism of the Chaldæan mysteries.

How the wryneck was first brought in, and finally assumed the chief place, is a puzzle. It reminds one of the story of the calf in the Vaidik rite, which so interfered with the sacred service of the sage that he had to tie it up to a post before he could continue the rite. This casual incident became finally sterotyped into the chief feature of the rite !

Certain it is that the Iynges of our Oracles have nothing to do with wrynecks ; we shall, therefore, make bold to translate them as Wheels or Starters.

They were presumably thought of as Living Spheres, whirling out in every direction from the centre, and swirling in again to that same centre, once they had reached the limit of their periphery or surround. They were also, in all probability, conceived of as Winged Globes—a familiar figure in Babylonian and Egyptian art—thus symbolizing that they were powers of the Air, midway between Heaven, the Great Surround, and Earth, the fixed Centre. In other words, they were the Children of the Æon.

An anonymous ancient writer tells us (K. 39) that it is the blending of the intellectual (or gnostic) and intelligible (or ideal) orders—that is, the union of the prototypes of what we distinguish as subject and object in the sense-world of diversity, or what we might call the self-reflective energy of the Mind on the plane of reality—that first " spirts forth " the One Iynx, and after this the three Iynges that are called "paternal"

12

and also " unspeakables." This writer also characterizes the Iynx as the " One in the three Depths after it " (it is, therefore, of an æonic nature), and says that it is this three-in-one hierarchy that divides the worlds into three—namely, empyrean, ætherial, and terrene.

The information of Damascius refines and complicates the idea, when he tells us that " the Mind of the Father is said to bring forward [on to the stage of manifestation] the triadic ordering— Iynges, Synoches, Teletarchæ "—which we may render tentatively as Whirlings, Holdings-together and Perfectings.

The Synoches we have come across before (i. 58). *Teletarchia* is used by ecclesiastical writers as a synonym of the Trinity; while Orpheus is called *teletárchēs* as the founder of mysteries or perfectionings.

The root-meanings underlying the names of the members of this triad seem to suggest, as we have already said, the ideas of creating (or preferably

13

starting), preserving (or maintaining), and completing (or perfecting or finishing).

Damascius thinks that the last words of the following two verses refer to the triad of the One Iynx.

*K.* 40.
*C.* 40.

*Many are these who leaping mount upon the shining worlds ; among them are three excellencies* [or *heights*].

The meaning of the first clause is doubtful. Who the many (fem. pl.) are, is not clear ; it may mean that there are hosts of subordinate Iynges. On the contrary, it may have nothing to do with these Nature-Iynges on the Path of Descent, that is the bringing into manifestation, but may refer to souls who in the Ascent win their way to the " shining worlds " or Worlds of Light, and become Iynges consciously

According to both Damascius and Proclus, the Order of Iynges is characterized as having the power both of

14

proceeding or going-forth and of drawing- together or contracting—that is, both of expansion and contraction, of out-breathing and in-breathing. They are, moreover, free Intelligences.

*The Whirls [Iynges] created by the* K. 40. *Father's Thought are themselves, too, intel-* C. 54. *ligent [or gnostic], being moved by Wills ineffable to understand.*

They are created by Divine Thought, as Sons of Will and Yoga, and procreate by thought ; they are Mind-born and give birth to minds. Their epithet is the " *Ineffables* " or " *Unspeakables* "; they are further called in the Oracles " *swift*," and are said to proceed from and to " *rush to* " or " *desire eagerly* " the Father (C. 52) ; they are the "*Father's Powers.*" Indeed, as Proclus declares :
" For not only do these three divinities [or divine natures] of themselves bring into manifestation and contract them [*sci.*, out of manifestation], but they are

15

also 'Guardians' [or Watchers or Pre-servers] of the 'works' of the Father, according to the Oracle—yea, of the One Mind that doth create itself " (K. 40, C. 41).

Iynx in its root-meaning, according to Proclus, signifies the "power of trans-mission," which is said, in the Oracles, "to sustain the fountains." The same idea seems to be latent in the following verse :

K. 40.
C. 64.

*For all cosmos has inflexible intelligent sustainers.*

The meaning is quite clearly brought out when Proclus, elsewhere, affirms that the Order of the Iynges "has a trans-missive [that is, intermediary or ferrying] power, as the Theologers call it, of all things from the Intelligible [or Typal] Order into Matter, and again of all things into it [sci., the Intelligible]."

In other words, they are the direct link between the Divine and physical,

16

and to some extent also suggest the idea of Angels or Messengers; yet are they like to Wheels and Whirls, or Vortices—on the one hand to vortical atoms, and on the other to individualities. They are, of course, in essence, quite unbound by ideas of extension in space, and sequence in time; though they manifest in space and time.

Porphyry preserves a curious Oracle which reads:

*With secret rites drawing the iynx from the æther.*   K. 41.

This Oracle, however, may have been taken from some Theurgist or Hellenized Magian source and not from our poem; and so also may the following quoted by Proclus:

*Be active [or operate] round the Hecatic spinning thing.*   K. 41. C. 194.

It is doubtful what *stróphalus* means

17

exactly. It may sometimes mean a top ; and in the Mysteries tops were included among the mystic play-things of the young Bacchus, or Iacchus. They represented, among other things, the " fixed " stars (humming tops) and planets (whipping tops).

The Iynx was said to be active, or to energize, on the three—empyrean, ætherial and terrene—planes.

## THE MAINTAINERS.

Though the Later Platonic commentators make two other allied hierarchies out of the Synoches and Teletarchæ, both these, as we have seen, should rather be taken as modes of this same mysterious Iynx. In manifestation, from one it passed to three, and so became many. Thus a scrap of our Oracles reads :

K. 41.
C. 57.

*Nay, and as many as are subject to the hylic* [or *terrene*] *Synoches.*

This would seem to mean simply the

Powers that hold together, or con-tract, or mass, material things ; and these Powers are again the Iynges, or simul-taneously creative, preservative, and destructive or perfective Intelligences of the Father-Mind, which are in the Oracles symbolically called His " *Lightnings* " when thought of as Rays or Intelligences. The word *Prēstēres* (Lightnings), however, is more graphically and literally rendered as Fiery Whirlwinds—like waterspouts. These are again our Iynges or Whirls or Swirls or Wheels, spinning in and out. Thus two verses read :

*But to the Knowing Fire-whirls of the* K. 42.
*Knowing Fire* [i.e., *the Father*] *all things* C. 63.
*do yield, subject unto the Father's Will*
*which makes them to obey.*

As we have seen above (p. 16) these Whirls, as Synoches—that is, in their power of holding together—were called " Guardians," and this is borne out by two verses :

*K.* 42.  
*C.* 56.     *He gave to His own Fire-whirls the power to guard the summits, commingling with the Synoches the proper power of His own Might.*

The " summits " suggest these self-same Iynges in their creative mode ; the series of which they were the " summits " being creative (or inceptive), preservative (or guardian), and perfective (consummative or regenerative).

Thus Damascius tells us that the whole Demiurgic Order—that is to say, the order of things in genesis—was surrounded by what the Oracles call the "*Fire-whirling Guard.*"   In brief it is the power of holding together (? gravitation on the life-side of things).

This is fundamentally the great power of the Mother-side of things ; for, as we have seen (i. 57), the Great Mother is :

*K.* 19.  
*C.* 99.     *Source of all sources, Womb that holds all things together.*

20

It follows, therefore, that the Iynges, as creative, are on the Father-side; as preservative (or Synoches) on the Mother-side; and as result or consummating or perfecting (or Teletarchæ) on the Son-side.

Damascius bears this out when he tells us that the Oracles call the Synoches the "*Whole-makers*" (*holopoioi*)—that is to say, they are connected with the idea of wholeness or oneness or the root-substance side of things, and again with the idea of the Æon.

Of course, the symbolic categories of Father, Mother, and Son are really all aspects of One and the same Mystery—the That which understands itself alone and yet is beyond understanding. To this Proclus refers when he writes (K. 42, C. 7): "Including [containing, preserving] all things in the one excellency [or summit] of His own subsistence, '*Himself subsists wholly beyond*,' according to the Oracle."

THE ENDERS.

So also with the Teletarchæ or Perfecting Powers; as Proclus tells us, they have the same divisions as the Synoches (and Iynges); that is to say, it is again all the same thing looked at from the Son-side of things. There was thus, in the elaboration of the Later Platonic commentators, a triple, and even a sevenfold, division of this order or hierarchy. Considering the Teletarchic energy, or activity, as triadic, Proclus tells us that in its first mode it has to do with the finest or ultimate substance, the Empyrean, and says that it plays the part of Driver or Guide to the " *foot* [?—tarsón] *of Fire* "—which may be simply a poetical phrase for the Fire in its first contact with substance. Its middle mode, embracing beginnings and ends and middles, perfects the Æther; while its third mode is concerned with Gross Matter (*Hylē*), still confused and unshaped, which it also perfects.

From these and other elaborations of a like nature, we learn that the Teletarchs

were regarded as three, and were in-timately bound up with the Synoches, and therefore with the Iynges (C. 58). The unifying or holding-together of the Synochic power is de-fined and de-limited by the perfecting nature of the Teletarchic power—

*Into beginning and end and middle things by Order of Necessity.*

In this connection it is of interest to cite a sentence from Proclus that is almost certainly quoted from the Oracles. It relates to the Ascent of the individual soul and not to cosmogenesis, to perfection in the Mysteries and not to the Mysteries that perfect the world :

*The Soul-lord, he who doth set his feet upon the realms ætherial, is the Per-fectioner [Teletarch].*

Finally, Proclus refers the following two verses to the Teletarchs :

23

*K. 43.*      *Nay, a Name of august majesty, and,*
*C. III.*    *with sleepless whirling, leaping into the*
*worlds, by reason of the Father's swift*
*Announcement.*

In another passage Proclus refers to the " *Transmissive* " Name that leaps into activity in the " *boundless worlds* " (K. 44); and in yet another passage (K. 40), which we have already quoted (p. 16), he gives this " Name " to the Iynges. This plainly refers to the " *Intermediaries who stand* " between the Father and Matter, as Damascius says (K. 44), who further affirms that in their aspect of Teletarchs they are perfecting, and rule over all perfections, or the perfecting rites of the Mysteries.

So much, then, for the highest Principles or Ruling Powers of the Sensible World. The commentators further speak of a division among the Gods into Gods within the Zones and Gods beyond the Zones; but no verse from the Oracles is extant by which we can control this statement. It seems to mean simply that they were classified according as to whether their operations were concerned with the Seven Spheres, or were beyond them.

## THE DAIMONES.

The lesser powers were, according to Olympiodorus, divided into Angels, Daimones and Heroes. Concerning the Heroes, however, we have no fragment remaining ; while Angels and Daimones are at times somewhat confused. On the Daimones we have the following two verses :

*Nature persuades us that the Daimones* K. 44.
*are pure, and things that grow from evil* C. 191.
*matter useful and good.*

Kroll thinks that this means that Nature deceives us into thinking that the evil Daimones are good ; it may, however, mean that whereas from Man's standpoint Daimones are good or evil,

25

according to Nature they are pure, or indifferent, or non-moral. Their operations are conditioned by man's nature. They are in themselves non-human entities, and there is a scale of them from lowest to highest.

## THE DOGS.

Certain classes of them the Oracles call " *Dogs* " ; and here we may quote an interesting passage from Lydus (K. 30) :

" Whence the tradition of the Mystic Discourse [? the Oracles] that Hecatē [the World-Mother] is four-headed because of the four elements. And the fire-breathing head of the Horse evidently refers as it were to the sphere of fire ; the bellowing head of the Bull has reference to a certain bellowing power connected with the sphere af air ; the bitter and unstable nature of the Hydra [or Water-serpent] is connected with the sphere of water ; and the chastening and avenging nature of the Dog with that of earth."

The last clause throws some light on the allied figure of Anubis in Egyptian psychopompy, and also on the following fragment of the Oracles :

*Out of the Womb of Earth leap Dogs terrestrial that unto mortal never show true sign.*    K. 45.  C. 97.

It is impossible to say what this means precisely without the context. " Dogs " are the intelligent guardians of the secrets of various mystery-traditions ; they are ever watchful. The Outer Guards of the Adyta in which the mystic rites were celebrated, were sometimes called Dogs. Much could be written on this symbolism, beginning with Anubis and the Dog-ape of Thoth (see " Dog " in the Index of *H.*). Dog was a name of honour in the Mysteries. The Pythagoræans called the Planets the " Dogs of Persephonē "; sparks were poetically called the " Dogs of Hephæstus." The Eumenides, were called " Dogs," and the Harpies " Dogs

27

of Great Zeus." Perhaps this may throw some light on our particular Oracle; in the Oracles generally, however, they seem to have been a generic name of apparently wider meaning than in the symbolism which Lydus uses; unless we assume that for him the earth-sphere extended to the moon, when it would have three " planes "—terrene, watery and aëry—each of which had its appropriate Dogs.

Thus Olympiodorus writes: "From the aëry spaces begin to come into existence the irrational Daimones. Wherefore also the Oracle says:"

K. 45.
C. 75.
*She [? Hecatē] is the Driver of the aëry and the earthy and the watery Dogs.*

Kroll refers to the last of these Dogs the epithet "*Water-walkers,*" which Proclus quotes from the Oracles in the following passage:

"'Watery' as applied to divine natures signifies the undivided domain over

28

water ; for which cause, too, the Oracle calls these Gods ' *Water-walkers* ' " (K. 45, C. 76).

It is clear, however, that this refers to a far higher " dominion " than that of the Dogs. These inferior Daimones had their existence as far as the Moon only, in what was regarded as the realm of the impure nature or gross matter. Beyond the Moon the Daimones were held to be of a higher and purer order ; these were also called Angels—a term that in all probability came into our Hellenized Oracles along the line of the Mago-Chaldæan tradition.

Psellus speaks of " *the manifoldly-flowing tribes* " (the group-soul idea) of the Daimones, and this phrase was in all probability taken from the Oracles. (K. 46). It would seem to indicate that the nature of the Daimones was unstable and Protean, or rather that they could assume any form at will.

## THE HUMAN SOUL.

We now come to the important subject of the doctrine of the Oracles concerning the human soul.

The soul, as we have already seen (i. 71), was brought into being by the union of three; it is a triad, or rather a monad united with a triad.

K. 26.
C. 81.

*Having mingled the Spark of soul with two in unanimity—with Mind and Breath Divine—to them He added, as a third, Pure Love, the august Master binding all.*

We must, then, suppose that the individual souls, as lives, flow forth from the World-Soul, the Great Mother; it is, however, the Father who conditions them by His Creative Thought.

K. 46.
C. -78.

*These things the Father thought, and [so] made mortal [man] to be ensouled.*

30

"Mortal man" here seems to mean man as conditioned by body. The Soul is, as it were, a middle term between Mind and Body—both for the Great World and for the little world, or man; for two verses run :

*The Father of men and gods placed Mind*    K. 47.
*in Soul, and Soul in inert Body.*    C. 18.

The fundamental distinction, however, between the Mind and Soul is not easy to draw with any great clearness. They may be thought of as Light and Life, the eternally united complements of the One Mystery, the masculine and feminine powers of the sexless Supreme. So also with the individual soul in man; the soul-spark is a light-spark which is also a life-spark, or rather life-flood; it is centre and sphere in perpetual embrace —for mind and soul are not to be separated, no man can put them asunder. The nature of this "soul" (*ātma-buddhi*) is immortal and divine.

31

K. 47.
C. 20.

*For Soul being shining Fire, by reason of the Father's Power, both keeps immune from Death, and body is of Life, and hath the fulnesses* [plērōmata] *of many wombs.*

In the cosmic process (and also in the case of the individual) when the Sea of Substance has been impregnated by the Beams of Light, the whole Sea changes from dull and sluggish Matter (*tamas*) to bright Soul (*sattva*). It has become one now instead of indeterminate, cosmic and no longer chaotic. It is now the Sea of Life, the complement of all imperfection.

It is in all probability to the individual Soul that Psellus refers, when he writes : " For if, according to the Oracles, it is ' *a portion of the Fire Divine,*' and ' *shining Fire,*" and ' *a creation of the Father's Thought,*' its form is immaterial and self-subsistent " (K. 47, n. 2).

## THE VEHICLES OF MAN.

The original text of our Oracle-poem had, probably, something to tell us of

32

other " vehicles " or " garments " of the Soul besides the gross body ; but no verses on this interesting subject are extant.

Proclus, however, tells us that the disciples of Porphyry " seem to follow the Oracles, in saying that in its Descent the Soul ' collects a portion of Æther and of Sun and Moon, and all the elements contained in Air.' " Compare with this the Oracle quoted above (i. 79) :

*O Æther, Sun, Moon's Breath, Leaders of Air.*        K. 33.
                                                       C. 136.

And also a fragment of Porphyry preserved by Stobæus :
" For when the soul goes forth from the solid body, there follows along with it the spirit which it collected from the spheres " (K. 47, n. 3).

And with this compare the following passage from the Trismegistic tractate " The Key " :
" Now the principles of man are this wise vehicled : mind in the reason, the

C        33

reason in the soul, soul in the spirit, and spirit in the body.

"Spirit pervading body, by means of veins and arteries and blood, bestows upon the living creature motion, and, as it were, doth bear it in a way. . . .

"It is the same for those who go out from the body.

"For when the soul withdraws into itself, the spirit doth contract within the blood, and soul within the spirit. And then the mind, stripped of its wrappings, and naturally divine, takes to itself a fiery body" (*H.*, ii. 149, 151).

And so also Proclus, treating of the Ascent or Return, and plainly referring to the Oracles, writes :

"In order that both the visible vehicle may, through the visible action of them [*sci.*, the Rays], obtain its proper treatment [or care], and that the vehicle that's more divine than this, may secretly be purified, and [so] return to its own proper lot, '*drawn upward by the lunar and the solar Rays*,' as says somewhere one of the Gods [*i.e.*, the Oracles]."

Compare with this the Pitṛi-yāna and Deva-yāna, or Way of the Fathers and Way of the Gods, in the Upanishads. This " more divine vehicle " was generally called by the Later Platonic school the " ray-like " (*augo-eidés*), or " star-like " (*astro-eidés*), or. "spirituous" (*pneumatik-ón*) body; and its purification and enlivening by means of the Rays are admirably set forth in the rubrics of the *Mithriac Ritual* (Vol. VI.).

## SOUL-SLAVERY.

In itself, the Soul is possessed of a divine nature, and is naturally free ; in the earth-state, however, it is now in slavery owing to its being drunk with the things of gross matter (*hylē*). This at any rate seems to be the meaning of the following three lines that have, unfortunately, been considerably mangled by the copyists :

K. 48.  *The Soul of man shall press God closely*
C. 83.  *to itself, with naught subject to death in*
*it ; [but now] it is all drunk, for it doth*
*glory in the Harmony beneath whose sway*
*the mortal frame exists*

With these lines are probably to be
taken the verse quoted above (i. 30) :

K. 15.  *Not knowing God is wholly God. O*
C. 184.  *wretched slaves, be sober !*

The Harmony is the system of the
Seven Formative Spheres of Genesis, or
Fate.  And so Proclus, speaking of Souls,
writes :
   " Which also the Gods [*i.e.*, the Oracles]
say are slaves when they turn to generation (*genesis*) ; but '*if they serve their
slavery with neck unbent*,' they are brought
home again from out this state, leaving
the state of birth-and-death (*genesis*)
behind."

36

## THE BODY.

As to body, the doctrine of the Oracles was, as with nearly all the mystic schools of the time, that of naïve ascetic dualism in general, that is if we can trust the commentators. Body seems more or less to have been identified with matter. It is said to be " in a state of flux," " spread out," and " scattered." It was apparently called, in the Oracles, the " *tumultuous vessel* " or " *vessel of tumult* "—the epithet being derived from rushing, roaring and dashing waves, and the idea being connected with the flowing nature of material things, presumably, as contrasted with the quiet of the contemplative mind.

Proclus speaks of " the earth from which one must '*lighten the heart*'" (K. 48), and this " heart " must be associated with what he calls, after the Oracles, " the '*inner heart*' in the essence of the soul " (K. 47, n. 1).

The unfortunate body is thus regarded as the " *root of evil*," or " *naughtiness*,"

37

and is said to be even the "*purgation of matter*" (K. 48), one of our extant fragments characterizing it plainly as the "*dung*" or "*dross of matter*" (K. 61, C. 147).

It may here be noted that in the *Pistis Sophia*, matter is called the "superfluity of naughtiness," and men (that is men's bodies) are said to be the "purgation of the matter (*hylē*) of the Rulers" (*P.S.*, 249, 251, 337) ; and it is very credible that this was one of the doctrines of the " Books of the Chaldæans."

Matter (*hylē*) is here not regarded as the fruitful substance of the universe, the " Land flowing with milk and honey," but as the dry and squalid element beneath the Moon, which, Proclus tells us, is called, in the Oracles, the "*unwatered*," that is in itself unfruitful, the Desert as compared with the Land of true living substance (K. 48).

NATURE.

In this gross matter dwells the body which is subject to Nature, that is Fate.

38

The physical body, then, appears to have been regarded as an excretion within the domain of Nature or the Fate-sphere. Psellus, accordingly, writes concerning the Soul, or rather the Light-spark :

" But the Gnostic Fire comes from Above, and is in need of its native Source alone [presumably, the true spiritual life-substance] ; but if it be affected by the feelings of the body, Necessity compels that it should serve it [the body] and [so] be set beneath the sway of Fate, and led about by Nature " (K. 48).

This suggests the putting on the " form of a servant," of the Pauline Letters (*Phil.*, ii. 7), and the Trismegistic " becoming a slave within the Harmony [*i.e.*, Fate-sphere] " (*H.*, ii. 10).

This gross matter, or hylic substance, extended as far as the Moon ; it constituted, therefore, practically the atmosphere, or surround, of the earth, generally spoken of as the sublunary region. The Moon was its " Ruler," being the " image " of the Great Mother, Nature, who conditions

39

all genesis—that is, becoming or birth-and-death. Speaking of this Lunar Sphere, which surrounds the hylic regions, Proclus tells us that in it were " the causes of all genesis " or generation; and quotes a sacred *logos* in confirmation :

K. 49.    *The self-revealed glory* [or *image*] *of Nature shines forth.*

Whether these words are quoted directly from our poem, is not quite certain ; it is, however, highly probable, for an isolated verse runs :

K. 49.    *Do not invoke the self-revealed image*
C. 148.   *of Nature.*

Here Mother Nature is what the Greeks called Hecatē, and her " image " or nature-symbol, or glory, is the Moon. Very similar to this is the fragment :

K. 49.    *Turn not thy face Naturewards* ; [*for*]
C. 149.   *her Name is identical with Fate.*

40

Perhaps the second clause has been defaced in the tradition ; it is difficult to make out the precise sense from the present text, unless it means simply, as Iamblichus tells us, that : " The whole being [or essence] of Fate is in Nature " —that is to say, that Nature and Fate are identical.

In close connection with this we must take the Oracular prohibition :

*Do not increase thy Fate !*

K. 50.
C. 153.

Fate may here be said to be the result of contact with many people and objects. Everything that we have intercourse with on earth enlarges our destiny, for destiny in this sense is the result of earthly happenings. We should, accordingly, seek within everything for further ideas, and not simply rush about and spread ourselves all over space. This seeking within by means of true mind is not stirring up the secret powers of Great Nature ; it is rather the understanding of Fate.

41

The prohibition thus seems to mean :
Do not increase the dominion of the body
of the lower nature, or rather the Moon-
ruled plasm.

Within the same range of ideas also, we
may, perhaps, bring the isolated apo-
strophe from the Oracles :

K. 50.
C. 94.
*O man, thou subtle handiwork of daring
Nature !*

This refers to the body of man that is
wrought by the Nature-powers, the ele-
mental intelligences of the Mother.

### THE DIVINE SPARK.

The " soul " is thus thought of, in this
doctrine, as struggling against the
" body " ; in this great Struggle, or
Passion, it is helped by the Father, who
has bestowed upon it a particle, or rather
portion, of His own Mind, the living
" *symbol*," or pledge, or token, of Himself. This struggle, or passion, is in
reality the travail, or birth-throes, of the

42

self-born Son. It is because of this Light-spark, by reason of this pledge, that souls fallen into generation, and therefore forgetful in time of their Divine origin, can recover the memory of the Father.

*For the Mind of the Father hath sown symbols through the world—[the Mind] that understands things understandable, and that thinks-forth ineffable beauties.*    K. 50.   C. 47.

Psellus has a variant of the first verse, namely :

*The Mind of the Father has sown symbols in the souls.*    C. 80.

These " symbols " are the seeds of Divinity (the *logoi* or " words " of Philo and the Christian Gnosis), but they are not operative until the soul converts its will from the things of Fate to those of Freedom, from self-will to spiritual free-will. On this we have, fortunately, three verses preserved :

43

*K. 50.*    *But the Mind of the Father doth not*
*C. 164.*    *receive her will, until she hath departed*
*from Oblivion, and uttereth the word, by*
*putting in its [Oblivion's] place the Memory*
*of the Fatherhood's pure token.*

On this Psellus comments : " Each,
therefore, diving into the ineffable depths
of his own nature, findeth the symbol of
the All-Father." " Uttering the word "
is, mystically, bringing this *logos*, or
light-spark, into activity.

**THE WAY OF RETURN.**

The Path of Return to the Father was
set forth at length in the Oracles, and on it
we have, fortunately, a number of fragments :

*K. 51.*    *Seek out the channel of the Soul-stream,*
*C. 172.*    *—whence and from what order is it that*
*the soul in slavery to body [did descend,*
*and] to what order thou again shalt rise,*
*at-one-ing work with holy word.*

44

The meaning of "word" in this and the preceding fragment is doubtful. We may either take it mystically, as we have suggested above, or it may be taken magically, as the utterance of compelling speech—in the lower sense, the theurgic use of invocations, and in the higher the utterance of true "words of power," that is the "speech of the gods" which is uttered by right action, or "work." This reminds us of the "Great Work" of the Alchemists, and of Karma-yoga, or the "union by works," of Vaidik theosophy, taken in the mystic sense and not the usual meaning of ceremonial acts. Kroll thinks that the "holy word" means the knowledge of the intelligible world of the Father, but I do not quite follow him.

## THE ARMOUR OF SOUNDING LIGHT.

The nature of the Quest is set forth mysteriously as follows :

*Armed at all points, clad in the bloom of Sounding Light, arming both mind and*    K. 51.
    C. 170.

*soul with three-barbed Might, he must set in his heart the Triad's every symbol, and not move scatteredly along the empyrean ways [or channels], but [move] collectedly.*

Compare with this (i. 87) :

K. 36.
C. 171.

*Yea, verily, full-armed without and armed within like to a goddess.*

This refers to the Re-generate, as described in the *Mithriac Ritual*. The "three-barbed Might" is taken probably from the symbol of the trident, and represents the triple-power of the Monad. As the *Ritual* says (page 27), he must hold himself steady and not allow himself to be "scattered abroad"; all his "limbs" must be collected, or gathered together, as the Osiris in resurrection. Compare with this *The Gnostic Crucifixion* (pp. 16, 52 ff.), and also the remarkable description of a somewhat similar experience in a story, by E. R. Innes, in *The*

46

Especially to be noticed is the graphic phrase "Sounding Light," showing that the close connection between colour and sound was known to the initiates of these mysteries. This Sounding Light, however, in its mystical sense, was probably the Uttered Word, or, to use another figure, the putting-on of the "Robe of Glory." Compare with this the Descent of the Eagle in the Hymn of the Soul of Bardaisan :

" It flew in the form of the Eagle,
 Of all the winged tribes the king-bird;
It flew and alighted beside me,
 And turned into speech altogether."

       (*F.*, p. 410).

This Sounding Light is thus the true "symbol" of the Paternal or Spiritual or Intelligible Monad. Proclus speaks of the intelligence as being "well-wheeled," by which he means smoothly spinning round a centre ; this centre being the Intelligible (K. 51). But, to our taste, this is by no means a good simile, for the Intelligible or Spiritual Mind embraces all things and is not a centre. Proclus, however, seems to base himself upon this verse :

K. 51.     *Urging himself to the centre of Sounding*
C. 126.  *Light.*

But when we remember the "three-barbed Might" of our first fragment above (K. 51, C. 170), we may, perhaps, be permitted to translate *kéntron* as "goad" :

*Urging himself on with the goad of Sounding Light.*

We thus bring the main idea into relation with the contemporaneous Trismegistic doctrine of the Master-Mind (*i.e.*, the Spiritual Mind) being the Charioteer, and driving the soul-chariot, with gnostic rays (or reins) that sound forth its true counsels. In any case the mystic should find no difficulty in transmuting the symbols, passing from centre to periphery or from periphery to centre as the thought requires.

Finally, with regard to the first quotation under this heading, it may be said that in re-generation man begins to re-clothe himself ; only when he makes these new clothes, they no longer bind but clothe him with power. The " bloom " (or vigour) of Sounding (or Resounding) Light is an armour that rays forth. " Might " (or Strength) suggests inner stability, that which is planted within and is the root of stability, the foundation. The ātmic, or spiritual, " spark," in the virgin soil, or womb, of the man's spiritual nature, is the Strength of the Father. It is the Power to stop chaos swirling, and so start the enforming or ordering of itself. Thus it is that the man starts making the symbols and sounds whereby his Name or Word is actualized.

THE WAY ABOVE.

Such a man should begin to know the nature of the regions unto which he is being brought, and so understand the mystic precept :

K. 51.
C. 174.

*Let the immortal depths of thy soul be opened, and open all thy eyes at once to the Above.*

It is proper to follow the " great " passions and desires of the soul, provided the "eye," or true centre of the mind, be fixed Above ; for then the passions are sure to be pure, and not personal attractions, not little bonds of feeling and sentiment.

This " opening of all the eyes " concerns the mystery of the Æon. In the Depths of the New Dawn every atom of the man must become an eye ; he must be " all eye." As vehicle of Sounding Light he must become an Æon—" a Star in the world of men, an Eye in the regions of the gods."

50

But to be clothed with this Royal Vesture, this Robe of Glory, he must strip off the " garb of the servant," the bonds of slavery, the " earthy carapace " :

*The mortal once endowed with Mind*    K. 52.
*must on his soul put bridle, in order that*    C. 175.
*it may not plunge into the ill-starred*
*Earth but win to freedom.*

" Endowed with Mind " is the Trismegistic " Mind-led." This Spiritual Mind, or Great Mind, is the Promethean, or Foreseeing, Mind in man (as Proclus tells us), who plays the part of Providence over the life of reason in us—that is, the rational man or animal—that this life may not be destroyed by being—

*Dowsed in the frenzies of the Earth and*    C. 190.
*the necessities of Nature.*

This is quoted by Proclus from our poem, for he adds : " As one of the Oracles says."
This " dowsing," or baptism, of the

soul in the waves of the Ocean of Genesis, or Generation, the Watery Spheres, is referred to several times in the Trismegistic fragments (K. 52, n. 1), and is the converse of the Spiritual Baptism or " Dowsing in the Mind," as we read in the Divine Herald's Proclamation, in the treatise called " The Cup " or " Mixing-bowl "—the Monad.

" Baptize thyself with this Cup's Baptism, what heart can do so, thou that hast faith thou canst ascend to Him who hath sent down the Cup, thou that dost know for what thou did'st come into being " (*H.*, ii. 87).

Of similar purport are the verses :

K. 52.
C. 160.

*Unto the Light and to the Father's Rays thou ought'st to hasten, whence hath been sent to thee a soul richly with Mind arrayed.*

" Hasten " is a mystery-word, suggesting activity without motion. The soul must be lightened and stripped of its gross garments of matter (*hylē*).

52

*For things Divine are not accessible* K. 52.
*to mortals who fix their minds on body;* C. 169.
*'tis they who strip them naked [of this*
*thing], that speed aloft unto the Height.*

These are the true Naked, the real
Gymnosophists, as Apollonius of Tyana
would have called them, who strip off
the " form of the servant," the rags of
the lower nature. Compare with this
the early Jewish commentator in the
Naassene Document, who was evidently
well versed in the " Books of the Chaldæans " :

" For this Mystery is the Gate of
Heaven, and this is the House of God,
where the Good God dwells alone ; into
which House no impure man shall come.
But it is kept under watch for the Spiritual
alone ; where, when they come, they
must cast away their garments, and all
become bridegrooms, obtaining their true
manhood through the Virginal Spirit "
(*H.*, i. 181).

If this transmutation be effected, and

the "rags" changed into the shining garments of the pure elements, the "wedding garments" of the Gospel parables, the soul by its own power wins its freedom. Such a man is characterized by Proclus as "having a soul that looks down upon body, and is capable of looking Above, '*by its own might*,' according to the Oracle, divorced from the hylic organs of sense" (K. 52).

## PURIFICATION BY FIRE.

The Path of Return, or Way Above, was conceived as a purification of the soul from the hylic elements, and therewith an entry into the purifying mystery of the Baptism of Fire, which in its highest sense is the "Dowsing" in the Divine Mind of the Trismegistic teaching.

K. 53.
C. 158.
*For if the mortal draw nigh to the Fire, he shall have Light from God.*

Speaking of the "perfecting purification," Proclus tells us that it was operated by means of the " *Divine Fire*," and that it was the highest degree of purification, which caused all the " *stains* " that dimmed the pure nature of the soul, through her converse with generation, to disappear. This he takes directly from the Oracles.

## THE ANGELIC POWERS OF PURIFICATION.

In this purification certain Divine Powers, or Intelligences, take part ; they are called Angels (Messengers or Mediators). They are the higher correspondence of the infernal Daimones in *The Vision of Aridæus* (pp. 33 ff.), in which the " stains " of the souls are graphically depicted.

The part played by these Intelligences, however, is not external to the soul, but an integral part of the transmutation ; it is the Angelic portion of the man that leads the soul Above.

It is this, as Proclus tells us, from the

55

Oracles, that "*makes*" the soul "*to shine with Fire*"—that is, which itself shines round the man on all sides; it rays-forth, becomes truly "astral" (*augo-eidés* or *astro-eidés*), rays-forth with intelligence.

It is this Angelic power that purifies the soul of gross matter (*hylē*), and "*lightens it with warm spirit*"—that is, endows it with a true impersonal or "cosmic" subtle vehicle, tempered by means of that "temperature" or "blend" which the *Mithriac Ritual* (p. 19) tells us depends entirely on the Fire.

The original poem seems, from Proclus' comments, further to have contained verses which referred to certain Angelic Powers who, as it were, made to indraw the external protrusions of the soul which it sympathetically projects in conformity with the configuration of the limbs of its earthy prison-house; their function, therefore, was to restore it to its pure spherical shape. To this may refer the very corrupt and obscure verse:

*The projections of the soul are easy to* K. 53.
*unloose by being inbreathed.* C. 88.

## THE SACRED FIRES.

Breath (Spirit) is said mystically to be
the Spouse of Fire (Mind); and so we
find Proclus speaking of " perfecting the
travail of souls and '*lighting up the Fire*' in
them," and also of "lighting up the fires
that lead them Home"; all of which, for
the mystic, can refer to nothing else than
the starting of what are called the "sacred
fires " of spiritual transformation. These
" fires " are intelligent transforming currents that re-form the soul-plasm into
the " perfect body," that is, the " body
of resurrection," as the *Mithriac Ritual*
(p. 19) informs us. And so we read :

*Extend on every side the reins of Fire to* K. 53.
[*guide*] *the unformed soul.* C. 173.

That is, constrain the flowing watery
nature of the soul by the fiery breath or
spirit of the true Mind. And this seems

57

also to be the meaning of the difficult fragment :

K. 54.
C. 176.

*If thou extendest fiery Mind to flowing work of piety, thou shall preserve thy body too.*

This seems to mean that, when by means of purification, and by dint of pious practices, the soul is made fluid—that is to say, is no longer bound to any configuration of external things, when it is freed from prejudice, or opinion, and personal passion, or sentiment, and is " with pure purities now purified," as the *Mithriac Ritual* (p. 20) has it—then this re-generated soul-plasm, the germ of the " perfect body," can be configured afresh according to the plans or symbols of the true Mind.

Then shall the re-generate souls have Gnosis of the Divine Mind, be free from Fate, and breathe the Intelligible Fire, thus understanding the Works of the Father.

*They flee the reckless fated wing of Fate, and*    K. 54.
*stay themselves in God, drawing unto them-*    C. 90.
*selves the Fires in all their prime, as they*
*descend from out the Father, from which, as*
*they descend, the soul doth cull the Flower*
*of Empyrean Fruit that nourisheth the soul.*

It is hazardous to say what this may mean with any great precision, for in all probability the text is corrupt in several places. Taking it as it stands, however, we may conjecture that the first line refers to the state of the souls in subjection to Fate; they are figured elsewhere as leaving the state of sameness and rest, and flying forth down into the hylic realms of Genesis, or repeated birth and death. This is winging the " shameless " (or reckless) " wing of Fate ; " and yet this too is " fated." They who return to the memory of their spiritual state, once more rest in God, and breathe in the " Gnostic Fires " of the Holy Spirit—the true Ambrosia, that which bestows immortality *(athanasia).*

THE FRUIT OF THE FIRE-TREE.

This Fruit of Life—that is, the Gnosis, or Gnostic Son of God—as may be seen from *The Great Announcement*, of the Simonian tradition, based on Mago-Chaldæan mystic doctrines (see *The Gnostic Crucifixion*, pp. 40 ff.), was figured as the Fruit of the Fire-Tree. The Church Father Hippolytus (*Ref.*, vi. 9) summarizes the original text as follows:

" And, generally, we may say, of all things that are, both sensible and intelligible, which he [the writer of the *Announcement*] calls Manifested and Hidden, the Fire which is above the Heavens, is the Treasure, as it were a Great Tree, like that seen by Nebuchadonosor in vision, from which all flesh is nourished.   And he considers the manifested side of the Fire to be the trunk, branches, leaves, and the bark surrounding it on the outside. All the parts of the Great Tree, he says, are set on fire by the devouring flame of the Fire and destroyed. But the Fruit of the Tree, if its imaging hath been perfected, and it takes the shape of itself, is placed in the Storehouse, and not cast into the Fire. For the Fruit, he says, is produced to be placed in the Storehouse, but the husk to be committed to the Fire ; that is to say, the trunk which is generated not for its own sake but for that of the Fruit."

See further my *Simon Magus* (p. 14). The original form of this *Great Announcement* is in all probability a pre-Christian document (see *H.*, 184, n. 4), for the early Jewish commentator in the Naassene Document is acquainted with it. Now in this Document the pre-Christian Hellenistic initiate writes :

" Moreover, also, the Phrygians say that the Father of Wholes is Amygdalos [*lit.*, the Almond-Tree]."

And this is glossed by the same Jewish commentator, who knew *The Great Announcement*, as follows :

" No ordinary tree ; but that He is that Amygdalos the Pre-existing, who, having in Himself the Perfect Fruit, as it were, throbbing and moving in His Depth, tore asunder His Womb, and gave birth to His own Son " (*H.*, i. 182).

## THE PÆAN OF THE SOUL.

But to return to the Oracles ; Proclus evidently bases himself upon a very similar passage to the last-quoted verses of our poem, when he writes :

" Let us then offer this praise-giving to God—the becoming - like - unto - Him. Let us leave the Flowing Essence [the River of Genesis] and draw nigh to the true End ; let us get to know the Master, let all our love be poured forth to the Father. When He calls us, let us be obedient ; let us haste to the Hot, and flee the Cold ; let us be Fire ; let us ' fare on our *Way through Fire.*' We have an ' *agile Way* ' for our Return. ' *Our Father is our Guide,*' who ' *openeth the Ways of Fire,*' lest in forgetfulness we let ourselves flow in a ' *downward stream* ' "
(K. 54).

The lust of generation is said to "moisten" the soul and make it watery; the Fire dries it and lightens it. The Hymn, or Praise-giving, which the souls sing on their Way Above is called by Olympiodorus, quoting most probably from the text of our poem, the "*Pæan*," or Song of Joy (C. 85); it is a continual praise-giving of the man who tunes himself into harmony with the Music of the Spheres. (See *The Hymns of Hermes*, pp. 17 ff., and 57 ff).

## THE MYSTERY-CULTUS.

The cultus of the Oracles is, before all else, the cult of Fire, and that, too, for the most part, in a high mystical sense rather than in the cruder form of external fire-worship. The Sacred Living Fire was to be adored in the shrine of the silence of the inner nature. These inner mysteries were in themselves inexpressible, and even the very method of approach, it seems, was handed on under the vow of silence.

Our poem was thus originally intended
to be an apocryphon (in the original sense
of the term), or esoteric document ; for
Proclus tells us that its mystagogy was
prefaced by the words :

K. 55.    *Keep silence, thou who art admitted to*
C. 51.    *the secret rites* [mýsta].

And elsewhere he says that the Oracles
were handed on to the Mystæ alone.
As a way of approach to the innermost
form of the rites, which was indubitably
a solitary sacrament like the *dynamis* of
the *Mithriac Ritual*, there was an inner
ceremonial cultus. Thus from one fragment we recover the following instruction
to the officiating priest :

K. 55.    *But, first of all, the priest who doth direct*
C. 193.   *the Works of Fire, must sprinkle with cold*
          *wave of the deep-sounding brine.*

There was, therefore, a ceremonial
ritual.   The   consummation   of   the

innermost rite, however, was solitary, and of the nature of a Mystic Union or Sacred Marriage.

## THE MYSTIC MARRIAGE.

Thus Proclus speaks of the soul, " according to a certain ineffable at-one-ment, leading that-which-is-filled into sameness with that-which-fills, making one portion of itself, in an immaterial and impalpable fashion, a receptacle for the in-shining, and provoking the other to the imparting of its Light." This, he says, is the meaning of the verse :

*When the currents mingle in consummation of the Works of Deathless Fire.*    K. 55.    C. 21.

## THE PURIFYING MYSTERIES.

But this can be accomplished only in the perfected body, or rather " perfect body "; therefore, with regard to visions of the lower powers, operated by the daimones, Proclus tells us :
" The Gods admonish us not to look

upon them before we are fenced round with the powers brought to birth by the Mystery-rites : "

K. 55.
C. 150.

*Thou should'st not look on them before the body is perfected ; [for] ever do they fascinate men's souls and draw them from the Mysteries.*

The lower visions were to be turned from in order that the higher theophanies, or manifestations of the Gods, might be seen. But this could be accomplished only by an orderly discipline. And so Proclus writes :

" For in contemplation and the art of perfectioning, that which makes the Way Above safe and free from stumbling-blocks for us, is orderly progress. At any rate, as the Oracles say : "

K. 56.
C. 183.

*Never so much is God estranged from man, and, with Living Power, sends him on fruitless quests—*

66

"As when, in disorder and in discord, we [try to] make the Ascent to the most divine heights of contemplation or the most sacred acts of Works—as it is said, '*with lips unhallowed and unwashen feet.*'"

## THE FIRE - GNOSIS.

Proclus further tells us that the first preliminary of this truly sacred cultus is that we should have a right intuition of the nature of the Divine, or, in the graphic words of the Oracles, a "*Fire-warmed intuition*" (K. 56) :

*For if the mortal draw nigh to the Fire,*    K. 53.
*he shall have Light from God.*    C. 158.

There must, however, be no rush or hurry, but calm steadfast perseverance, for it is all a natural growth. Therefore is it said that :

*For the mortal man who takes due time*    K. 56.
*the Blessed Ones are swift to come into being.*    C. 158.

67

This, however, does not mean to say that the man should be slow; for:

K. 56. *A mortal sluggish in these things spells the dismissal of the Gods.*

This is explained by an interesting passage of Damascius, who, speaking of the mysterious "instrument" the *iynx*, writes: "When it turns inwards, it invokes the Gods; and when outwards, it dismisses those it has invoked." Mystically this seems to mean that when the "whirl"—or vortex "instrument" of consciousness, or the one-sense "perfect body"—turns inwards, theophanies, or manifestations of the Gods, appear; and when it turns outward, to the physical, they disappear.

## THE MANIFESTATIONS OF THE GODS.

In themselves the Gods have no forms, they are incorporeal; they, however, assume forms for the sake of mortals, as Proclus writes : "For though we [the Gods] are incorporeal : "

*Bodies are allowed to our self-revealed manifestations for your sakes.*    K. 56. C. 106.

This self-revelation, which in one mode signifies the selection of some image in the seer's own mind, and in another, connotes the seeing by one's own light, pertains to the mystery of that monadic Light which transcends the three lower (empyrean, ætherial and hylic) planes or states (K. 31). And Simplicius further informs us (K. 57), quoting from Proclus : " This, he says, is the Light which first receives the invisible allotments of the Gods, and for those worthy makes manifest in itself the self-revealed spectacles. For in it, he says, according to the Oracle : "

*The things that have no shape, take shape.*    K. 57. C. 114.

This seems to be the Astral Light

proper, "cosmic" and not personal. To this interpretation of Proclus', however, Simplicius objects that, according to the Oracles, the impressions of typical forms, or root-symbols, and of the other divine visions, do not occur in the Light, but are rather made on the æther´ (C. 113). We, however, need not labour the point further than to remark that Proclus had wider personal experience of those things than Simplicius. The things seen in the Great Light were true, for this Light constituted the Plane of Truth, whereas the ætherial was a reflection, and was further conditioned by the personality of the seer. Proclus, therefore, tells us that :

"The Gods [*i.e.*, presumably the Oracles] warn us to have understanding of '*the form of light that they display*'" (K. 57, C. 159).

In another passage Proclus refers to the mystic experience of these theophanies on the empyrean plane, where shapes of fire are assumed : " The

70

tradition of these [visions] is handed on THE CHALDÆAN ORACLES.
by the mystagogy of the tradition of the
Gods ; for it says : "

*When thou hast uttered these [? words of*    *K.* 57.
*power], thou shalt behold either a fire*    *C.* 198.
*[? flame] resembling a boy, dancing upon*
*the surface of the waves of air [? æther] ;*
*or even a flame that hath no shape, from*
*which a voice proceeds ; or [yet] a wealth*
*of light around the area [of sight], strident,*
*a-whirl. Nay, thou shalt see a horse as*
*well, all made of fire, a-flash with light ;*
*or yet again a boy, on a swift horse's back*
*astride,—a boy clad all in flame, or all*
*bedecked with gold, or else with nothing on ;*
*or even shooting with a bow, and standing*
*on horse-back.*

With the above may be compared
the symbolic visions in *A Mithriac
Ritual* (pp. 27, 32) ; we have here evidently to do with the same order of
experiences, and so also in the following
four verses :

*K. 57.*
*C. 196.*
*If thou should'st oft address Me, thou shalt behold all things grow dark ; for at that hour no Heaven's curved dome is seen ; there shine no Stars ; Moon's light is veiled ; Earth is no longer firm ; with Lightning-flash all is a-flame.*

In connection with the idea underlying the phrase "a flame that hath no shape, from which a voice proceeds," of the last fragment but one, we must take the lines :

*K. 58.*
*C. 199.*
*But when thou dost behold the very sacred Fire with dancing radiance flashing formless through the depths of the whole world, then hearken to the Voice of Fire.*

### THE THEURGIC ART.

But to reach this pure and formless vision was very difficult ; for all kinds of false appearances and changing shapes could intervene. These had to be cleaned from the field of vision, for they were held to be due to impure presences, or,

72

as we should prefer it, to the impurities of the man's own lower nature. On this subject our Oracles (though more probably it is an interpolation from a Theurgic tradition) had instruction, as we learn from the curious fragment :

*But when thou dost perceive an earth-ward daimon drawing nigh, make offering with the stone* mnouziris, *uttering [the proper cnant].*

K. 58.
C. 196.

What this stone may have been, we have no knowledge. To " make offering " with a stone can mean nothing else than to put it into the fire, and this should connect with alchemy. *Mnouziris* is a *barbarum nomen.*

The chant, or *mantra*, would also consist of *barbara nomina* (native names), concerning which Psellus quotes the famous lines that are generally referred to our Oracles, but which, for reasons of metre, could not have stood as part of the poem (C. 155) :

73

"See that thou never change the native names; for there are names in every nation, given by the Gods, possessed of power, in mystic rites, no language can express."

In this Theurgy, or "Divine Work," moreover, certain symbols, or symbolic figures, were employed, for Proclus says (K. 58) that the Oracles "call the angular points of the figures '*the compactors.*'"

## THE ROYAL SOULS.

But Theurgy was not for all; it was the Royal Art, and could be practised with spiritual success only by those whom the Trismegistic writers (*H.*, iii. 125) would have called Royal Souls. Their nature is set forth in the following verses, preserved by Synesius :

K. 58.
C. 86.

*Yea, verily, indeed, do they at least, most happy far of all the souls, pour down to Earth from Heaven; most blest are they with fates* [lit., *threads*] *no tongue can tell, as many as are born from out*

74

This is evidently a reference to the Race, the Sons of God. (See *The Gnostic Crucifixion*, pp. 48 ff.). So also does the Orphic initiate declares : " My Race is from Heaven."

There may be some slight doubt as to whether the above fragment is from our poem, for Synesius does not say from what source he takes his quotation ; but short of the precise statement everything is in favour of its authenticity, and especially the following from the same philosophic and mystical Bishop :

## THE LIGHT-SPARK.

" Let him hear the sacred Oracles which tell about the different ways. After the full list of inducements [or promptings] that come from Home to cause us to return, according to which it is within our power to cause the

75

inplanted Seed to grow, they continue : ''

*To some He gave it to receive the Token of the Light, to others, even when asleep, He gave the power of bearing Fruit from His own Might.*

The " Token of Light " is evidently the " Symbol " that the Father implants in souls. It is the Seed of Divinity, the Light-spark, that gradually flames forth into the Fire. This Light-spark was conceived of as a seed sown in good soil that could bear fruit, thirty, or sixty or a hundred fold, as the Christianized Gnosis has it.

And so in the Excerpts from the lost work of the Christian Gnostic Theodotus, made by the Church Father Clement of Alexandria, we read (K. 59) : " The followers of the Valentinian doctrine declare that when the Psychic Body hath been enformed, into the Elect Soul in sleep the Masculine Seed is implanted by the Logos."

76

If the soul can pronounce its own true Word (Logos), utter its Sound, and so create by itself symbols, then may the man hope really to understand what his consciousness may catch from the highest spheres. But even if his soul cannot do this, even while it is unaware of its surroundings, and without this creative power, it is still possible that it may be able to catch some of the Strength and Might (not Light) of the Father-Mind, and thus be inspired to conceive some true ideas.

The re-generated soul is said to become a " Five-fold Star," as we learn from the *Mithriac Ritual* (p. 24), and also from Lydus (*De Mens.*, 23.6), who tells us that : " The Oracle declares that souls, when restored to their former nature by means of this Pentad, transcend Fate."

*For Theurgists are not counted in the herd subject to Fate.*　　K. 59.
　　　　　　　　　　　　　　　　　　　　C. 185.

And so also Proclus tells us that :

"We should avoid the multitude of men that go '*in herds*,' as says the Oracle."

The "herd" has, so to speak, got only one "over-soul" between them,— they do not yet stand alone; or, rather, they have a soul each, and only one "over-mind" between them.

Those of the "herd" are the "processions of Fate" of the Trismegistic writings (*H.,* iii. 273); while those who have perfected themselves, are freed from the Wheel of Fate, and become Angels or Gods. Speaking of the man who is truly devoted to sacred things, Proclus quotes an Oracle which says :

*K.* 60.    *Alive in power he runs, an Angel.*

**THE UNREGENERATE.**

On the contrary, the unregenerate is characterized as :

*K.* 60.    *Hard to turn, with burden on the back, who has no share in Light.*

78

While concerning those who " lead an evil life," Proclus tells us that the Oracles declared :

*For as for them they are no great way*   *K*. 60.
*off from Dogs irrational.*

Of such a one it is said :

*My vessel the Beasts of the Earth shall*   *K*. 60.
*inhabit.*   *C*. 95.

Compare with this the Gnostic Valentinian doctrine, as summarized by Hippolytus :
" And this material man is, according to them, as it were an inn, or dwelling-place, at one time of the soul alone, at another of the soul and daimonian existences, at another of the soul and words (*logoi*), which are words sown from Above —from the Common Fruit of the Plērōma (Fulness) and Wisdom—into this world, dwelling in the body of clay together

79

with the soul, when daimons cease to cohabit with her " (*F.*, p. 352).

And also the Basilidian doctrine, as summarized by Clement of Alexandria :

" The Basilidians are accustomed to give the name of appendages [or accretions] to the passions. These essences, they say, have a certain substantial existence, and are attached to the rational soul, owing to a certain turmoil and primitive confusion.

" Onto this nucleus other bastard and alien natures of the essence grow, such as those of the wolf, ape, lion, goat, etc. And when the peculiar qualities of such natures appear round the soul, they cause the desires of the soul to become like to the special natures of these animals, for they imitate the actions of those whose characteristics they bear " (*F.*, pp. 276, 277).

## THE PERFECTING OF THE BODY.

The physical body was called in the Oracles the " dung of matter," as we have

80

seen above (p. 38), and as we may see from the obscure couplet :

*Thou shalt not leave behind the dung of matter on the height; the image* [eidōlon] *also hath its portion in the space that shines on every side.*

This seems to mean either that the higher states of consciousness were not to be contaminated and befouled with the passions of the body, or that in the highest theurgy the body was not to be left behind in trance, but, on the contrary, that conscious contact was to be kept with it throughout the whole of the sacred operation, as we learn from the *Mithriac Ritual*. The " image " also—presumably the image - man, or subtle vehicle of the soul, the *augoeidēs* or *astroeidēs*—had an important part to play in linking the consciousness up with the Light-world.

In this connection we may also take the lines already quoted above (p. 58) :

F        81

*K.* 54.     *If thou dost stretch thy fiery mind unto*
*C.* 176.    *the flowing work of piety, thou shalt pre-*
              *serve thy body too.*

What the " flowing work of piety "
may be, it is hazardous to say. It is
probably a poetical expression for the
pure plastic substance out of which the
" perfect body " was to be formed, as set
forth in the *Mithriac Ritual.* The work
of the " fiery mind " is thus described in
the Trismegistic sermon " The Key " :
" For when the soul withdraws into
itself, the spirit doth contract itself
within the blood, and soul within the
spirit. And then the mind, stript of its
wrappings, and naturally divine, taking
unto itself a fiery body, doth traverse
every space " (*H.,* ii. 151).
And again :
" When mind becomes a daimon, the
law requires that it should take a fiery
body to execute the services of God "
(*H.,* ii. 154).
And here we may append a passage

from Julian the Emperor-Philosopher, THE CHALDÆAN ORACLES.
who loved our Oracles :

"To this the Oracles of the Gods bear witness ; and [therefore] I say that, by means of the holy life of purity, not only our souls but also our bodies are made worthy to receive much help and saving [or soundness] ; for they declare : "

*Save ye as well the mortal thing of bitter matter that surrounds you.*   K. 61.
C. 178.

For the mystery-term "bitter matter" see the note in the *Mithriac Ritual* (pp. 41 ff.). Kroll thinks that all this refers to the dogma of the resurrection of the physical body, but the Ritual makes it plain that the only "body of resurrection" with which the Mystics and Gnostics were acquainted, was the "perfect body" ; the resurrection of the gross physical body was a superstition of the ignorant.

The "dung of matter" referred to above may be rendered as "dross" or

83

" scum," and a somewhat more mystical interpretation might be suggested. " Dross " as a mystery-word is essentially the same as " scum," but from an analytical point of view suggests the reverse of " scum." Certain states of the soul may be spoken of as scum ; in spiritual alchemy when the soul-plasm is thought of as the " watery " sphere being gradually dried, so as to be eventually built up, or enformed, by the " fire " of the spiritual mind, then the scum rises to the top and is handed over to Fate. Scum would then mean men under the bondage of Fate. Dross, however, suggests the earth or metal side of things, and here the refuse falls and does not rise, and is again handed over to further schooling and discipline, and not allowed freedom from the law, like jewels and pure earth are.

Scum and dross are on the matter-side of things ; images may be said to correspond to them on the mind-side. As scum is to the soul, as dross to pure matter, so is image to pure mind. Both

84

scum and image have to do with the
surface of things and not with the depth.

## RE-INCARNATION.

As we might expect, the Oracles taught the doctrine of the repeated descents and returnings of the soul, by whatever name we may call it, whether transmigration, re-incarnation, palingenesis, metempsychosis, metensomatosis, or transcorporation. And so Proclus tells us that :

" They make the soul descend many times into the world for many causes, either through the shedding of its feathers [or wings], or by the Will of the Father " (K. 62).

The soul of a man, however, as also in the Trismegistic doctrine (*H.*, ii. 153, 166), could not be reborn into the body of a brute ; as to this Proclus is quite clear when he writes :

" And that the passing into irrational natures is contrary to nature for human souls, not only do the Oracles teach us,

85

when they declare that '*this is the law from the Blessed Ones that naught can break*'; the human soul :"

K. 62.    *Completes its life again in men and not in beasts.*

### THE DARKNESS.

There was also in our Oracles a doctrine of punishment in the Invisible (Hadēs); for Proclus speaks of "the Avenging Powers (*Poinai*), '*Throttlers of mortals*,'" and of a state of gloom and pain, below which stretched a still more awful gulf of Darkness, as the following verses tell us :

K. 62.
C. 145.    *See that thou verge not down unto the world of the Dark Rays, 'neath which is ever spread the Deep [or Abyss] devoid of form, where is no light to see, wrapped in black gloom befouling, that joys in shades [eidōla], void of all understanding, precipitous and sinuous, for ever winding*

86

*round its own blind depth, eternally in marriage with a body that cannot be seen, inert [and] lifeless.*

With this description of the Serpent of Darkness, ever in congress with his infernal counterpart of blind Matter and Ignorance, may be compared the vision of the Trismegistic " Man-Shepherd " treatise :

" But in a little while Darkness came settling down on part of it, awesome and gloomy, coiling in sinuous folds, so that methought it like unto a snake " (*H.*, ii. 4.).

This is a vision of the other side, or antipodes, of the Light ; and so we find Proclus writing : " For this region is '*Hater of the Light*,' as the Oracle also saith " (K. 63). Also with regard to the system thought to underlie the Oracles, Psellus informs us that below the Æther come three hylic worlds or planes of gross matter—the sublunary, terrene, and sub-terrene—" the uttermost of which is

87

called chthonian and '*Light-hater*,' and is not only sublunary, but also contains within it that matter (*hylē*) which they call the '*Deep*.'"

**THE INFERNAL STAIRS.**

In connection with the above fragment we must also take the following corrupt lines, which evidently form part of the directions given to the soul for its journey through Hades :

K. 63.
C. 159.

*But verge not downwards! Beneath thee lies a Precipice, sheer from the earth, that draws one down a Stair of seven steps, beneath which lies the Throne of Dire Necessity.*

The topography of the Throne of Necessity corresponds somewhat with that in Plato's famous Vision of Er— which was probably derived from an Orphic mystery-myth ; and the old Orphic tradition was in contact with "Chald-dæan" sources. So also in the Vision of Aridæus, which again is perhaps connected with Orphic initiation, it is Adrasteia, Daughter of Necessity, who presides over the punishments in Tartarus, and her dominion extends to the uttermost parts of the hylic cosmos, as we learn from a fragment of a theogony preserved by Jerome (K. 63).

Proclus also speaks of the whole generative or genesiurgic Nature—that is, Nature under the sway of Necessity—in which, he says, is " both the ' *turbulence of matter* ' and the ' *light-hating world*,' as the Gods [*i.e.*, the Oracles] say, and the ' *sinuous streams*,' by which the many are drawn down, as the Oracles tell us."

Moreover, there must have been mention of some roaring or bellowing sound that struck the evil soul with terror, as in the Vision of Er ; for Psellus quotes a mutilated fragment, which runs :

" *Ah ! Ah !* " *the Earth doth roar at them, until* [*they turn*] *to children* (?). K. 63.

89

We may, however, venture to suggest another point of view from which the above symbolic imagery (K. 62) can be regarded, and take it not as a warning to ordinary fate-full people, but as an admonition to those who are being initiated or re-generated, and who can thus begin to stand aside from the Fate-spheres.

The " Precipice," or Gulph, could thus be regarded as the way of descent from the Light and the Fulness into the Fate-spheres, and so the organ or instrument of creation of darkness and " flat " things (shades). The soul descends by means of a " flat " ladder of planes, the way of the formal mind.

The admonition thus seems to say : Do not let the mind travel down into the Fate-spheres by means of " planes " and formal ideas, and the ordinary surface view of things ; because if so, it is apt to leave some of itself behind. There is a way of descending direct and straight into, or rather fathoming, the uttermost

Depths quite safely, but it is by way of living creatures, and not by way of mind-made ladders.

In mystical language " Throne " is the point of stability ; it suggests contact with the Stable One. This plan of seven, the ladder or root of form, is essentially stable and not vital ; and for an initiate who is on the return journey, active in the mystery of re-generation, it is to be avoided, as it leads back into imprisonment ; it is the proper way down, but not the right way back. It leads to states dominated by Fate, to a prison or school where the soul is bound all round with rules ; it does not lead to Freedom.

## ON CONDUCT.

We may now conclude with some fragments concerning right living ; in the first place with the famous riddle :

*Soil not the spirit, and deepen not the plane !*   K. 64.   
C. 152.

The first clause is generally thought to refer to the spiritual, or rather spirituous, body, while the second is supposed to mean : " Turn not the plane into the solid "—that is to say, if we follow Pythagoræan tradition : Do not make the subtle body dense or gross.

From a more mystical point of view it might be suggested that normal Nature is but as a superficies. Until a man is initiated properly, that is to say, naturally re-generated, it is better for him not to delve into her magical powers too soon, but rather keep within the plane-side of things till his own substance is made pure. When pure there is nothing in him to which these magical powers can attach themselves. As soon as his nature is purified then Spiritual Mind begins to enter his " perfect body," and so he can control the inner forces, or forces within, or sexual powers of Nature — those creative powers and passions which make her double herself. The superficial side of Nature is complete in its own way, and normal man should be content with this ; he should not attempt to stir the secret powers of her Depth, or Womb, till he is guided by the wisdom of the Spiritual Mind.

In the Latin translation of Proclus' lost treatise *On Providence*, the following three sayings are ascribed to the Oracles (*Responsa*). Kroll, however, thinks that the second only is authentic :

*When thou dost look upon thyself, let fear come on thee.*  K. 64.
C. 181.

*Believe thyself to be out of body, and thou art.*

*The spawning of illnesses in us is in our own control, for they are born out of the life we lead.*

If the man regards his own lower self, he fears because of his imperfection ; if he gazes on his higher self, he feels awe. With the second aphorism compare

93

the instruction of the Trismegistic treatise " The Mind to Hermes " (§ 19) :

" And, thus, think from thyself, and bid thy soul go unto any land, and there more quickly than thy bidding will it be " (*H.*, ii. 186).

**THE GNOSIS OF PIETY.**

That the spirit of the doctrine of the Oracles was far removed from the practice of the arts of astrology, earth-measurement, divination, augury, and the rest, and turned the mind to the contemplation of spiritual verities alone, may be seen from the following fine fragment :

*K.* 64.
*C.* 144.
*Submit not to thy mind the earth's vast measures, for that the Tree of Truth grows not on earth ; and measure not the measure of the sun by adding rod to rod, for that his course is in accordance with the Will eternal of the Father, and not for sake of thee. Let thou the moon's rush go ; she ever runs by operation of*

*Necessity. The stars' procession was not brought forth for sake of thee.*

*The birds' wide-winging high in air is never true, nor yet the slicings of the victims' entrails. These are all toys, lending support to mercenary fraud.*

*Flee thou these things, if thou would'st enter in True Worship's Paradise, where Virtue, Wisdom, and Good-rule are met together.*

There is somewhat of a Jewish Sibylline flavour about this which might seem to indicate contact with Jewish Gnostic circles. As, however, there is nothing else in our fragments which shows signs of Jewish influence, we may fairly conclude that the ethic of our Oracles was similar, and that similarity does not spell plagiarism.

Moreover the phaseology is identical with that of other fragments which can lie under no suspicion of a " Judaizing " influence ; for instance (i. 81 ; ii. 69) :

95

K. 34.   *Both lunar course and star-progression.*
C. 144.  *This star-progression was not delivered from the womb of things because of thee.*

K. 56.   *Bodies are allowed our self-revealed*
C. 186.  *manifestations for your sakes.*

And so we bring these two small volumes to a close in the hope that a few at least of the many riddles connected with these famous Oracles may have been made somewhat less puzzling.